Essential
California

by Richard Minnich

Richard Minnich comes from a long line of
serious travellers. Bitten by the travel bug at an
early age, he is fortunate to have seen a good bit
of the world. To him, writing about his travels is
fulfilling and a welcome diversion to his life as a
writer/producer of theatre and film. Essential
California is his first guidebook. Originally from
Pennsylvania, he currently resides in
Los Angeles.

Above: *mural on Ocean Front Walk, Venice Beach*

AA Publishing

Written by Richard Minnich

Edited, designed and produced by AA Publishing.
© The Automobile Association 1998
Maps © The Automobile Association 1998
Reprinted Nov 1998; Reprinted Apr 1999
Reprinted May 2001

Distributed in the United Kingdom by AA Publishing,
Norfolk House, Priestley Road, Basingstoke,
Hampshire, RG24 9NY.

A CIP catalogue record for this book is available from
the British Library.

ISBN 0 7495 1617 8

Above: *Frog Jumping Jubilee, Angel's Camp*

Page 1: *mural at Venice Beach*

Page 5a: *sculpture on Rodeo Drive, Los Angeles*

Page 15a: *parking on Rodeo Drive*

Page 27a: *cable-car, San Francisco – a fun way to travel around the city*

Page 91a: *City Lights bookstore, North Beach*
91b: *Fisherman's Wharf is the place to go for fresh seafood in San Francisco*

Page 117a: *T-shirts at Venice Beach*
117b: *having fun on the Boardwalk at Santa Cruz, a traditional American seaside resort*

Find out more about AA Publishing and the wide range of services the AA provides by visiting our Web site at www.theAA.co.uk.

Published by AA Publishing, a trading name of Automobile Association Developments Limited, whose registered office is Norfolk House, Priestley Road, Basingstoke, Hampshire, RG24 9NY.
Registered number 1878835.

Colour separation: BTB, Digital Imaging, Whitchurch, Hampshire

Printed and bound in Italy by Printers Trento srl

Contents

About this Book

Essential *California* is divided into five sections to cover the most important aspects of your visit to California.

Viewing California pages 5–14
An introduction to California by the author
  California's Features
  Essence of California
  The Shaping of California
  Peace and Quiet
  California's Famous

Top Ten pages 15–26
The author's choice of the Top Ten places to see in California, each with practical information.

What to See pages 27–90
The four main areas of California, each with its own brief introduction and an alphabetical listing of the main attractions.
  Practical information
  Snippets of 'Did You Know…' information
  4 suggested walks
  4 suggested tours
  2 features

Where To... pages 91–116
Detailed listings of the best places to eat, stay, shop, take the children and be entertained.

Practical Matters pages 117–24
A highly visual section containing essential travel information.

Maps
All map references are to the individual maps found in the What to See section of this guide.
For example, Alcatraz has the reference ➕ 29D6 – indicating the page on which the map is located and the grid square in which the island is to be found. A list of the maps that have been used in this travel guide can be found in the index.

Prices
Where appropriate, an indication of the cost of an establishment is given by **£** signs:
£££ denotes higher prices, **££** denotes average prices, while **£** denotes lower charges.

Star Ratings
Most of the places described in this book have been given a separate rating:
✪✪✪   Do not miss
✪✪   Highly recommended
✪   Worth seeing

Viewing
California

Above: *sculpture on Rodeo Drive, Los Angeles*

Richard Minnich's California

Describing California and its people is like trying to describe a beautiful painting: most people will have a different perspective and feeling. The word that most readily comes to mind is *extreme*. Nowhere on earth can one find such extreme variances of scenic splendour or inhabitants. Within an 80-mile span are the highest and lowest elevations in the United States, each with its own unique beauty.

From the very first person to set foot in the state to its most recent émigré, the trait that has most greatly characterised the state's populace is a deep commitment to adventure. California seems to define the concept of diversity with both its geography and inhabitants. With nearly every culture represented throughout the state, there are enough dining and entertainment selections to suit everyone's desire.

The Living Desert, a 1,200-acre garden and wild animal park in Palm Desert

California offers virtually every type of terrain, from desert to ocean to mountain, and environments ranging from small farming communities to giant metropolises that teem with cultural activity 24 hours a day.

If you're simply looking for rest and recuperation on your vacation, this is the place to visit. California is the epitome of 'laid back', even in its busiest cities. At the same time the state is the nation's leader for fashion and fun.

So often when travelling, one's preconceived notion of a destination and the reality of that destination vary greatly. But whatever your most romantic visions of California might be, rest assured your visit to this kaleidoscopic state will not disappoint. It is almost impossible to overestimate the grandeur that awaits.

California's Features

Geography
- Population: 31,800,000.
- Land area: 158,693 square miles.
- Highest point: Mount Whitney (14,494 feet).
- Lowest point: Death Valley (282 feet below sea level).
- Capitol: Sacramento.

Economic Factors
- California is the leading agricultural economy in the US, primarily because of its fruit crops: prunes, oranges, grapes, peaches, apricots, figs, lemons, avocados, dates, nectarines and rice plums. Other agriculture products include cotton, walnuts, almonds, sugar beet, tomatoes, eggs, turkeys, sunflowers and honey.
- Napa and Sonoma valleys (► 88) are famous for their wineries. Southern California has both film and television production and manufactures military aircraft and missiles.

Sports and Leisure
- Almost every conceivable sport, from boating and other watersports to sky-diving and rollerblading.

Animal Life
- The Pacific Ocean is home to humpback whales, sea otters, seals, sea lions, dolphins, elephant seals, and blue whales, the largest mammals in the world, as well as hundreds of species of smaller fish. The pupfish (desert sardine) has even managed to survive in arid Death Valley (► 71).
- Land animals include bison, deer, Roosevelt elk, mountain goats, big-horn sheep, mountain lions, bobcats, wild burros and black bear.
- Desert creatures include iguanas, chuckawallas, pronghorn antelope, coyotes, kangaroo rats and various insects and reptiles, including the dangerous black widow spider and the poisonous rattlesnake.
- Birdlife ranges from the exotic white-faced ibis and the tiny hummingbird to the bald and golden eagle and the mundane sea gull.

Plants
- Unique trees in California are the eucalyptus, sequoias, redwoods, Joshua trees and many varieties of palm. Various cacti and flowers also abound year-round.

Climate
California is known for its diversity of climates. Generally speaking, the south is warmer and the north cooler. The bay areas are renowned for their fog. The mountainous areas are known for pleasant summers and snowy winters at the higher elevations. The San Joaquin and Sacramento valleys are extremely hot during the summer months and cool and foggy the rest of the year. As a rule, most parts of the state are cool in the evenings, especially the coastal areas.

USC Trojans in the Coliseum

Essence of California

One of the best things about California is that you rarely have to plan your vacation around the seasons. If you wish to relax on the beach, accommodation ranges from luxurious oceanside resorts to basic camping facilities. If you want continuous entertainment, the state abounds with theme parks, fairs and festivals.

For the explorer or seeker of beauty, the natural habitat is varied and unbeatable. For a relaxing tour of the coastline, the Amtrak rail system runs from the top to the bottom of the state and features plush, picture-windowed lounge cars. Great for the photographer.

Bottom: *Zabriskie Point, Death Valley National Monument*

THE **10** ESSENTIALS

If you only have a short time to visit California, or would like to get a really complete picture of the state, here are the essentials:

• **Take a drive (or train)** along California's famous Route 1 for fantastic ocean views to the west and spectacular rolling hills and majestic mountain ranges to the east.

• **Spend the day** at one of the many beaches. Surf, sun or rent a bicycle, surfboard or rollerblades.

• **Walk across the Golden Gate Bridge** (► 19) from San Francisco to Marin County. Spend an hour or so wandering about the small towns on the other side, then walk or hop on public transport back to San Francisco. Finish the day with a cable-car ride to view the city's marvellous architecture.

• **Spend a day hiking or backpacking** in one of the many national or state parks. The Joshua Tree National Monument is an especially good one (► 73).

• **Experience the excitement** of professional sports in San Francisco, San Diego or Los Angeles or attend a horse race at one of the major tracks.

• **Go window-shopping** along Beverly Hill's exclusive Rodeo Drive (► 48, 49) or El Paseo Drive in Palm Springs (► 107).

• **Take a drive through the Napa Valley** wine country, stopping at any of the wineries for a tour and some wine-tasting (► 88). This is also an excellent place to buy your souvenirs to take back home.

• **Visit a theme park.** Disneyland is the most well-known (► 18), but Balboa Park/San Diego Zoo is exciting too (► 16).

• **Take the one-day cruise** from San Pedro or Newport Beach across to Catalina Island (► 17).

• **Tour one of Hollywood's** motion picture studios for an inside look at the making of screen magic. Universal Studios (► 54) is the most famous.

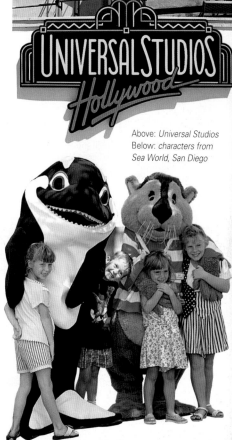

Above: *Universal Studios*
Below: *characters from Sea World, San Diego*

The Shaping of California

c7,000 BC
La Brea Tar Pit woman, first known LA resident, dies mysteriously.

AD 1542
Juan Cabrillo enters 'the Bay of Smokes' (San Pedro Bay).

1579
Sir Francis Drake claims San Francisco Bay area for Queen Elizabeth I.

1769
Franciscan monk Junípero Serra founds Mission San Diego de Alcala.

1777
Monterey becomes capital of Spanish-controlled California.

1781
Pueblo de Los Angeles is founded by 44 settlers of European, African and Native American heritages.

1790
Los Angeles population reaches 139.

1821
Spain grants independence to California.

1846
President Polk tries to purchase California (including parts of the present-day New Mexico) from Mexico for $40 million. Mexican-American War begins; US flag raised in San Francisco and Los Angeles.

1847
Yerba Buena, whose population is just a few hundred, is renamed San Francisco.

1848
James Wilson Marshall discovers gold at Coloma.

1849
Gold Rush attracts over 300,000 prospectors. San Jose becomes state capital.

1850
California joins the US as its 31st state.

1853
Levi Strauss creates denim jeans in San Francisco; Don Matteo Keller plants the state's first orange trees.

1854
Sacramento becomes the state capital.

1857
Fort Tejon earthquake (8.0) rocks Los Angeles.

1858
Wine industry is born.

1862
Telegraph connects San Francisco and New York.

1869
Railroad joins the east and west coasts.

1873
First cable-car in San Francisco. University of California established at Berkeley.

1881
First *Los Angeles Times* rolls off the presses. First snowfall in downtown LA.

The San Francisco earthquake of 1906

1882
First LA telephone directory is a mere three pages long.

1906
Earthquake and fire levels most of San Francisco.

1907
George Feeth introduces surfing to Southern California.

1908
Colonel William Selig opens first Hollywood film studio to produce *In the Sultan's Power*.

1915
Telephone connects New York and San Francisco.

1927
Charles Lindbergh's *The Spirit of St Louis* is built by Ryan Airlines in San Diego.

1929
First Academy Awards presentation at the Hollywood Roosevelt Hotel.

1933
Donald Douglas builds first mass-produced commercial aircraft, the DC-2, at Santa Monica.

1935
Statewide irrigation system turns the arid central valley plains into a lush green oasis.

1936
San Francisco-Oakland Bay Bridge opens.

1937
Golden Gate Bridge opens.

1940
First western freeway, 6-mile Arroyo Seco Parkway, opens in LA.

1942
Japanese shell Santa Barbara.

1945
United Nations signs charter in San Francisco.

1947
Anti-Communist hearings lead to Hollywood black-listing.

Marilyn Monroe

1955
Disneyland opens.

1960
Candlestick Park (now 3Com Park) opens in San Francisco.

1962
California becomes the most populous state in America.

1963
Marilyn Monroe dies.

1964
Beatles play Hollywood Bowl.

1968
Senator Robert Kennedy assassinated at LA's Ambassador Hotel.

1977
Silicon Valley develops Apple II, first marketable personal computer.

1980
Ronald Reagan, actor and ex-California Governor becomes US president.

1984
California hosts Summer Olympics.

1989
Earthquake (7.1) shakes San Francisco. Zsa Zsa Gabor arrested for slapping a Beverly Hills cop.

1992
Worst rioting in American history in Los Angeles after verdict in the police-beating trial of Rodney King.

1995
Jury acquits O J Simpson for the murders of Nicole Brown Simpson and Ronald Goldman.

1998–2000
California celebrates 150 years since the discovery of gold, the gold rush and the state's creation.

11

Peace & Quiet

Rarely can you visit an area and have so many options to choose from to amuse and entertain yourself, but in California there are also as many choices that offer nothing but relaxation and reflection in tranquil surroundings.

Southern California

Separate from the mainland, the picturesque Channel

Rock-climbers are often seen scaling the smooth granite boulders at Joshua Tree National Monument

Islands National Park and Catalina Island (▶ 17) provide a respite from the hustle and bustle of the city. Biking and horseback riding are offered on the islands, and both are wonderful for hiking.

Back on the mainland, in Santa Monica Mountains National Recreation Area hiking trails abound, and the coastline views are incredible from Sandstone Peak, its highest elevation at 3,111 feet. Nearby Point Dume is a popular secluded beach great for winter-time whale-watching. For nature at its best, visit the undeveloped Crystal Cove State Park near Laguna Beach and Torrey Pines State Reserve near La Jolla, in San Diego.

If you enjoy the desert, Anza-Borrego Desert State Park (▶ 82) and Lost Palm Oasis in Joshua Tree National Monument (▶ 73) provide incredible hiking and camping. As the ocean calms with its cascading sound and magnetic emanations, the desert soothes with unremitting sun and vast stillness. The extreme heat and dryness attract numerous birds, mammals and reptiles as well as intriguing plant life. Campgrounds are scattered throughout, many amid great climbing rocks, if you tire of merely sitting.

Central California

Gaviota State Park, Refugio State Beach and El Capitan State Beach, all in Santa Barbara County, offer perfect alternatives to the more crowded outdoor areas. After some quiet time on the beach, explore the hills and hiking trails just a short distance away.

Near Carmel, the Point Lobos State Reserve offers spectacular views of the Monterey cypress. Relax in the sun or take a more strenuous 50-mile bicycle ride through the Carmel Valley.

Northern California

If you like to hike, head for the Lost Coast Trail in Humboldt County. Just south of Eureka, the King Range National Conservation Area is a favourite with backpackers. Coastal redwoods and Roosevelt elk can be seen in abundance in the Prairie Creek Redwoods State Park. In the Shasta area, the Trinity Alps Wilderness offers great trails, or if you'd rather ride, there are exotic llamas for hire. In the Sierra Nevadas, the best hiking is in the aptly named Desolation Wilderness near Lake Tahoe (► 75).

Rock-climbers swear that scaling the granite face of such towering spires as El Capitan, in Yosemite National Park (► 26), is both invigorating and relaxing at the same time.

Gardens

If you don't want to leave the metropolitan areas, you can still escape by visiting one of the many botanical gardens in the state. The Self-Realization Centres in both Los Angeles and San Diego provide peaceful gardens in which to meditate. One little-known area is the Greystone estate (now a park) just off Doheny Drive, above Sunset in Los Angeles. The Asian temples of the major cities are also quiet spots, and many are surrounded by beautiful Zen gardens.

Stowe Lake, Golden Gate National Park

The Beach

Take some time out to experience the beach side of the Golden State. Nap on one of the many strands, or better yet, spend a night or two at a beachside hotel. Let the roar of the Pacific Ocean drown out civilisation's daily annoyances and the sun recharge your solar batteries. Add to this the gentle sea breezes through your hair, and the refreshing feel of salt water on your body.

13

California's Famous

One of Hollywood's most famous sons: John Wayne

Film and Television
Hollywood has created hundreds of celebrities, from Marilyn Monroe to John Wayne. Director Francis Ford Coppola and George Lucas, of *American Graffiti* and *Star Wars* fame respectively, are both Northern Californians who have set a standard for excellence in the film industry.

Music
Jerry Garcia, leader of the Grateful Dead, inspired the San Francisco music scene of the 1960s, which rocketed such musicians as Janis Joplin and The Jefferson Airplane to stardom. Jim Morrison, poet and singer for the Doors, was a student at UCLA film school and is considered one of the great musicians to emerge from Southern California. And you can't mention California music without including the Beach Boys, who captured Southern California's surf lifestyle with their music.

Literature
Dashiell Hammett, author of *The Maltese Falcon*, was a native Californian, and Beat Generation hero Jack Kerouac claimed San Francisco as his adult home (► 38). Jack London hails from Glen Ellen in Sonoma Valley (► 88), and John Steinbeck was born in Salinas (► 85).

Explorers
John Muir, founder of the Sierra Club, considered California paradise, and 1856 presidential candidate John C Fremont understandably preferred exploring California to politics. Who wouldn't?

Politics
Two 20th-century US presidents emerged from the state: Richard Nixon and Ronald Reagan. Nixon is remembered for his scandal-caused resignation and Reagan was the first actor elected to the highest office in the nation.

Business
Media mogul William Randolph Hearst (► 20), E W Scripps, founder of United Press International, and Orville Redenbacher, the popcorn king, all hail from the state.

Scandal
Author/humorists Artemus Ward, Bret Harte, Mark Twain, Ambrose Bierce and Joaquin Miller hung out together in 1860s San Francisco. Their friend, Adah Menken, scandalised the city by appearing in Byron's *Mazeppa* wearing nothing but a flesh-coloured body suit. She was strapped backwards on a horse as it galloped up a three-storey stage mountain complete with waterfalls and chasms.

Top Ten

Above: *parking on Rodeo Drive*

1
Balboa Park

Balboa Park, the pride of San Diego

This immense expanse of parks and museums includes the world-renowned San Diego Zoo.

A 100-tone chime serenades from the 200-foot California Tower, creating an exquisite backdrop for the historical buildings, museums and gardens of this 1,000-acre park. Start your visit from the main thoroughfare, El Prado (The Promenade). Here you'll find original exhibit halls from the 1915 Panama–California International Exposition, most notably the Casa del Prado. The Timken Art Gallery, a few blocks south, has interesting Russian icons among its exhibits.

At the park's centre are several small museums: San Diego History Museum, Photographic Arts Museum, Model Railroad Museum and Hall of Champions (sports). The nearby Reuben H Fleet Space Theater and Science Center provides hands-on exhibits for youngsters. The Natural History Museum features exhibits of southwest desert and marine life, and at the end of the plaza are The Museum of Man (► 61) and the San Diego Museum of Art.

Visit any of the three theatres of The Simon Edison Centre to see contemporary or Shakespearean plays, or enjoy a summer musical at The Starlight Bowl.

Simply stated, the **San Diego Zoo** (► 111 for practical information) is among the finest zoos in the world. The 100 acres simulate the natural habitats of the 800 species living here, and allows expansive roaming of its 3,500 animals, which include the only pair of pandas in the US. The Children's Zoo offers close-up views. There are guided bus tours, as well as an aerial tramway that rises 170 feet over the zoo's grottoes and mesas, providing a fine overview of the park.

✝ 59B2

✉ 1 mile north of downtown San Diego

☎ 619/239 0512

🕐 Daily 9–4

🍴 Restaurants, stands (££)

🚌 7, 7A or 7B from downtown

♿ Excellent

✋ Moderate

❓ Visitor Center sells multi-day passports to the park; free in-park tram

16

2
Catalina Island

Known as 'The Island of Romance', Santa Catalina Island is a perfect blend of relaxed resort, pristine shoreline and untouched wilderness.

Discovered in 1542 by Juan Rodriguez Cabrillo, Santa Catalina (commonly called Catalina Island) is roughly 26 miles from the mainland. One of the eight California Channel Islands, it is 21 miles long and 8 miles wide. No cars are allowed on the island, so use the public transport or rent the electric golf carts and bicycles available.

In 1811, the indigenous Gabrileño Indians were forced to resettle on the mainland, leaving the island that later became the private property of the Wrigley family, the chewing gum heirs. Today, 86 per cent of the island is owned by the non-profit Santa Catalina Island Conservancy, established in 1972 to preserve the island's natural beauty. The island provides a welcome retreat from mainland crowds, with its silent beaches, water sports, picturesque pier and deep-sea fishing.

The 1929 Avalon Casino is the most famous building on the island, best known for its art deco ballroom, which in its heyday was host to many of the world's most famous orchestras and big bands. The Catalina Island Museum, on the ground floor of the Casino, features exhibits on the island's history. The Wrigley Mansion, with its botanical gardens, and the Avalon Pier, in the middle of Avalon Bay, provide spectacular views of the interior hills and the breathtaking shoreline.

✚ 69D1

✉ Visitors Center, Green Pier

☎ 310/510 1520

🕐 Daily 8–5

🍴 Restaurants (£££)

🚢 Catalina Express 310/519 1212 or 800/995 4386; 1 hour each way; hourly from San Pedro or Long Beach.
Catalina Passenger Service 714/673 5245; 75 minutes each way; departs from Balboa Pavilion 9, returns 4:30

✈ Helicopter Service from Air Island Express 310/510 2525; 15 minutes each way

🖐 Travel moderate; exhibits cheap

Cruise ship at Catalina Island

3
Disneyland

Disneyland sets the standard for theme parks. This 'happiest place on earth' attracts 12 million visitors each year.

Children and adults alike are enchanted by the illusion and entertainment of 'magic kingdom', opened in 1955. The 76-acre park is divided into eight sections, offering such diverse attractions as fantasy rides, musical performances, parades, restaurants and shops.

The turrets and spires of Sleeping Beauty's Castle

© Disney Enterprises, Inc.

 69D1

 1313 Harbor Boulevard, Anaheim

714/781 4565

Mon–Fri 10–6, winter; 9PM weekends, holidays and summer; 9AM–midnight, 1AM Saturday

 Very good; free strollers and wheelchairs

 Expensive

 Hours and prices subject to change; on busy days park at the Disneyland Hotel and ride the monorail to the park

A series of pastel-coloured walkways lead from the central plaza at the end of Main Street USA into the various themed areas, each with their own rides, exhibits and excitement. Mickey's Toontown brings out the kid in everyone; Adventureland offers a jungle boat ride, the treehouse from *Swiss Family Robinson* to clamber about and the charming 'Tiki Room'. New Orleans Square has a Mississippi steamwheeler, the 'Pirates of the Caribbean' attraction and the 'Haunted Mansion'.

In Frontierland, you can careen down Thunder Mountain on a runaway train or raft across to Tom Sawyer's Island. Critter Country is the home of the 'Splash Mountain' flume ride and Country Bear Playhouse. Fantasyland begins when you cross the moat to Sleeping Beauty's castle, while Tomorrowland explores the future with such attractions as 'Space Mountain' and 'Star Tours'. For the courageous, the 'Indiana Jones Adventure' takes you on a trek to the Temple of the Forbidden Eye. Disney characters roam the streets and are happy to pose for pictures.

4
Golden Gate Bridge & National Recreation Area

The Golden Gate Bridge is quite easily the most beautiful and easily recognised bridge in the world.

The rust-coloured symbol of the West Coast stands as a beacon at the entrance of San Francisco Bay. Built in 1937 it is beautiful and impressive from any angle. Often cloaked in fog, the bridge is extraordinarily graceful and delicate in design even though its overall length is 8,981 feet, and the stolid towers reach 746 feet high.

Connecting San Francisco to Marin County and northern California, the suspension bridge withstands winds of up to 100mph and swings as much as 27 feet. Enjoy the drive over, or walk across for a truly spectacular perspective.

Golden Gate Park, the largest urban national park in the US, covers 74,000 acres from San Mateo County to Tomales Bay. The giant recreation area offers numerous attractions, including Fort Mason on San Francisco's waterfront. A former military embarkation point for soldiers during World War II, today the fort is the site of museums, theatres, galleries, restaurants and the last unaltered, operational liberty ship, the SS *Jeremiah O'Brien*.

The Golden Gate Promenade is a scenic bayshore hike stretching 3½ miles from Hyde Street Pier to Fort Point and beyond, across the Golden Gate Bridge. Among other sights in this impressive area are The Presidio, Baker Beach, Cliff House, Ocean Beach and Fort Funston, most of which are accessible by San Francisco's MUNI system.

✚ 28B5

Golden Gate Bridge

📻 MUNI 28; bus info 415/362 6600

♿ Excellent

✋ Free northbound; southbound toll, cheap

❓ Alcatraz tour info 415/546 2700

Recreation Area

✉ GGNRA, Building 201, Fort Mason, San Francisco, CA 94123

📞 415/556 0560 (information line)

🕐 Mon–Fri 9:30–4:30

🍴 Cafés, stands (£)

♿ Excellent

✋ Moderate

Instantly recognisable – Golden Gate Bridge

5
Hearst Castle

68C2

✉ 750 Hearst Castle Road, San Simeon

☎ 805/927 2020 or 800/444 4445

🕐 Daily 8:30–3. Five tours offered daily

♿ Excellent

✋ Moderate

❓ 214 miles southeast of San Francisco; 242 miles northwest of Los Angeles; parking just off Hwy 1 with shuttles buses to the castle. Four tours, priced separately. Tour 1 is recommended for first-time visitors. Reservations suggested

A rich man's castle – William Hearst's dream come true

William Randolph Hearst's tribute to excess and grandiosity crowns a hillside above the village of San Simeon.

The history of this fabulous castle dates back to 1865, when George Hearst purchased 40,000 acres of Mexican land adjacent to San Simeon Bay. His son, newspaper magnate William Randolph, began the castle when he took possession of the land in 1919, which now numbers 250,000 acres. Using steamers and chain-driven trucks to transport materials to the remote location, the palatial residence was not fully completed until 1947.

Casa Grande, as the mammoth mansion is called, boasts more than 100 rooms filled with priceless objects of art and antiques. It is one of seven estates owned by William Randolph, and was donated to the California Park Service in 1957.

Among the mansion's unique attributes are gothic fireplaces, Renaissance paintings (displayed in one of the 19 sitting rooms) and ceilings ranging in style from 16th-century Spanish to 18th-century Italian. In its prime, the doge's suite was reserved for the most important guests: presidents, visiting heads of state such as Winston Churchill and Hollywood luminaries. Marble colonnades and statuary flanking the indoor and outdoor pools replicate figures of antiquity.

There are also five greenhouses with over 700,000 annuals providing year-round colour, tennis courts and a movie theatre (in which Walt Disney hosted the first screening of *Snow White* in 1938). There are also two libraries, riding stables and the world's largest private zoo.

6
Hollywood

A one-time cow town, Hollywood is now the film-making capital of the world and trend-setting centre of glamour, glitter and excess.

The name that has drawn many a starry-eyed hopeful

Hollywood Boulevard is a relatively short street, but is one of the best known of all Los Angeles thoroughfares. Its wealth of art deco architecture has elevated it to the status of national historic district. From the 1920s to the 1950s, Hollywood boasted some of the country's largest movie palaces and exclusive department stores. As the movie industry expanded outward, Hollywood lost its lustre, but the faded star is now staging a comeback.

The Hollywood Roosevelt Hotel (▶ 101), site of the first Academy Awards, has been renovated and displays historical film memorabilia throughout. An ambitious three-block redevelopment project around Sid Grauman's 1927 Chinese Theatre (now Mann's Chinese) offers shops, cinemas, restaurants and the Hollywood Studio Museum.

Hollywood abounds with guided bus tours of every sort. Walking tours of its bronze-starred Walk of Fame are extremely popular. Begun in 1960 with only eight stars, there are now close to 3,000 celebrity prints. The 1920s Hollywood sign can best be viewed by venturing up Beachwood Canyon on the eastern edge of Hollywood or from Griffith Observatory, high atop Mount Hollywood.

Paramount Studio provides a peek into the world of film-making. Free tickets to several popular TV shows are readily available outside Mann's Theatre or through the major network studios.

Hawkers along Sunset and Hollywood Boulevards offer surprisingly accurate maps to celebrity homes at a low price; you can drive yourself or take a bus tour.

✚ 46B4

✉ Hollywood Visitors Bureau, 6333 W 3rd Street

☎ 213/624 7300; 213/937 3361 (LA TOURS); 213/469 8311 (Hollywood Chamber of Commerce)

🍴 Numerous restaurants, some open 24 hours (£–£££)

7
Monterey Peninsula

✠ 68B3

✉ 122 miles southeast of San Francisco; 334 miles northwest of LA

☎ 831/655 6450 (Visitors Bureau); 831/649 7118 (State Historical Park); 408/624 2522 (Carmel Bus Association); 408/625 5107 (Steinbeck Country Tours)

🍴 Various restaurants (££)

🚌 Monterey–Salinas Transit

✋ Cheap

'This is the California men dreamed of years ago. The face of the earth as the Creator intended it to look.' Henry Miller

For more than 300 years the Monterey Peninsula has enchanted everyone who has seen it. Formed by the Monterey and Carmel bays, the peninsula juts into the Pacific Ocean 120 miles south of San Francisco. Pristine beaches, craggy rock formations and wind- and wave-warped cypresses make the area among the most popular scenic spots in the world.

Nowhere in California is the state's Latin heritage more prevalent than in Monterey, where its exquisitely restored adobe buildings give testimony to the Spanish and Mexican periods of California history.

From art galleries in Carmel (► 71) to the grand estates in the dense woods of the Del Monte Forest, the scenic 17-Mile Drive through the forest between Pacific Grove and Carmel is almost incomparable in beauty.

The legacy of famed California author John Steinbeck can be traced at The Steinbeck Memorial Museum in Monterey (open daily). You can also visit his preserved cottage in nearby Pacific Grove.

Monterey Beach

Carmel-by-the-Sea is an enchanting village. Much of its architecture is reminiscent of rural European and early California styles. Monterey's Fisherman's Wharf has a magnificent promenade of fish markets, shops and theatres. For a different perspective, a sail can be arranged aboard the restored tall ship *Californian*.

Established at the turn of the century by a group of writers and artists, Carmel was originally a planned resort. As its popularity soared, it took on the reputation of something completely different: an exclusive bohemian retreat. Resisting efforts for modernisation, Carmel has preserved its idyllic setting. At Point Lobos State Reserve, two miles south of Carmel, harbor seals, gray whales and California sea lions frolic among a variety of sea birds and pelicans, a sight seen nowhere else in the world.

Sea lions are a familiar sight at Monterey

8
Napa Valley

Only 30 miles long and three miles across at its widest, this little valley boasts some 220 wineries.

Yountville, in the Napa Valley, is an important centre of wine production

68B4

✉ Visitor Information Center, 1310 Napa Town Center, Napa, 94559

☎ 707/226 7455 (Visitor Information Centre) 707/253 2111; 800/427 4124 (Napa Valley Wine Train)

🕐 Hours vary; some tours require reservations

🍴 Restaurants in the towns (£–££)

✋ Free–cheap

Leader of the American wine industry, the Napa Valley boasts such well-known names as Robert Mondavi, Domaine Chandon, Beringer and Sterling. Although the greatest concentration of wineries is along State Route 29, north from Napa to Calistoga, knowledgeable travellers use the Silverado Trail, a scenic, vineyard-lined parallel road along the eastern edge of the valley.

The city of Napa is the largest, although each of the valley towns has its charms. In Calistoga there are spas and geysers, one of which shoots 60 feet into the air every 40 minutes. St Helena claims many of the region's best dining and lodging choices, as well as a wine library and the Silverado Museum. An ancient volcanic eruption from Washington's Mount St Helens around 3 million years ago caused the giant redwoods of California to become instantly petrified. You'll find the Petrified Forest between Calistoga and Santa Rosa.

Outside of these towns lie more wineries, markets, inns, quiet picnic areas and historic parklands. Most visitors tour the vineyards, which offer a look at the wine-making process and feature wine-tastings, but there are also five different walking tours of the incredible architectural highlights of the valley (maps available at the information centre). If possible, avoid the crowded summer weekends. Many vintners now charge a small fee for the tastings and a few require reservations.

9
Redwood National Park

A vast forest of giant redwoods grows naturally nowhere else in the country except in this coastal region.

Before California's famous gold rush, and the resulting surge of new population, the world's tallest trees blanketed an area 30 miles wide and 450 miles long. The majority of today's redwood 'stands' are along US 101, from Leggett north to Crescent City. It is about a five-hour drive from San Francisco to the southern edge of the Redwood Forest, via the scenic coastal highway.

A small segment of old growth redwoods and outstanding coastal scenery have been protected in the 106,000-acre Redwood National Park. Eight miles of shoreline roads and more than 150 miles of trails afford close-up encounters with these magnificent trees and the abundant plant and animal life they nurture.

The three main state parks within the Park's boundaries are Prairie Creek, Del Norte Coast and Jedediah Smith. Campers favour Prairie Creek because of its herds of native Roosevelt elk and expansive beach (Gold Bluffs Beach). Lady Bird Johnson Cove is especially beautiful. Don't miss the Libby Tree, the tallest known tree, which towers to over 368 feet.

A drive through Del Norte Coast park allows you to enjoy spectacular ocean views and the inland forest simultaneously. The giant redwoods grow closest to the shoreline at the Damnation Creek Trail. In the spring, this area is the best place to view the abundant growth of rhododendrons and azaleas.

At the north end of the park, the Jedediah Smith terrain gives you an elevated perspective.

✚ 68B6

✉ National Park Headquarters, 1111 Second Street, Crescent City, 95531

☎ 707/445 7651 (Redwood National Park Information Center)

🍴 Restaurants (£); picnic facilities

✋ Moderate

Giant redwood – one of the world's largest trees

10
Yosemite National Park

✚ 69D4

✉ Yosemite Valley Visitors Center

☎ 209/372 0200

🕐 Apr–May, 9–6; Jul–Aug, 8–8; Sep–Oct, 8–6; Nov–Mar, 9–5

🍴 Restaurants (£)

✋ Moderate

Winter lends its own special majesty to Yosemite National Park

> *By any standards, Yosemite is the most spectacular national park in the country. To call it awe-inspiring would be an understatement.*

Nearly 70 per cent of the annual visitors to Yosemite National Park arrive in the summer and stay within the compact but awesome Yosemite Valley. The main section of the park, just 7 square miles in area, boasts monumental granite walls and high-diving waterfalls, but there remains almost 1,200 square miles of splendour to explore. Beyond are such natural wonders as giant sequoias, alpine meadows, lakes and trout-filled streams, Glacier Point and majestic 13,000-foot Sierra Nevada peaks. Giant sequoias are located in the Mariposa Grove, near the park's south entrance, about 30 miles from Yosemite Valley. In this great forest, over 200 trees measure more than 10 feet in diameter.

Some of the park's finest scenery is in the wild back country along the Tioga Road. There are rustic lodges and campgrounds (permit camping). In the main valley, 3,500-foot El Capitan attracts climbers from around the world.

Off-season visits are also spectacular. In autumn, leaves turn from green to crimson and gold and nights are cool and pleasant. Spring offers magnificent waterfalls that create rainbows across the valley floor. For the ambitious, there's the 200-mile John Muir Trail that follows the naturalist's path through the wilderness.

For many, the winter provides solitude and restores the raw grandeur of the park. The ski season at Badger Pass lasts from the end of November until mid-April.

What To See

Above: cable-car, San Francisco –
a fun way to travel around the city

27

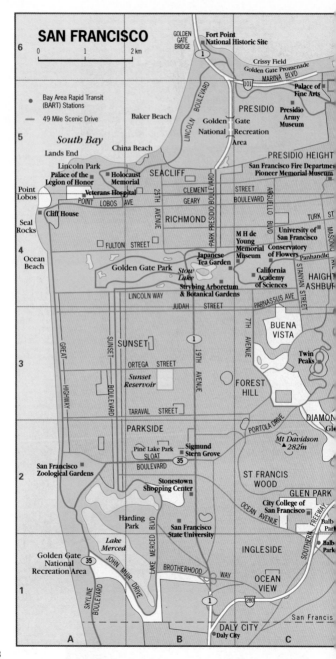

SAN FRANCISCO

0   1   2 km

● Bay Area Rapid Transit (BART) Stations
— 49 Mile Scenic Drive

GOLDEN GATE BRIDGE
■ Fort Point National Historic Site
Crissy Field
Golden Gate Promenade
MARINA BLVD

■ Palace of Fine Arts

PRESIDIO
■ Presidio Army Museum

South Bay
Lands End

Baker Beach

LINCOLN BOULEVARD

Golden Gate National Recreation Area

PRESIDIO HEIGHTS

China Beach

Point Lobos

Lincoln Park
■ Palace of the Legion of Honor
■ Holocaust Memorial
SEACLIFF

San Francisco Fire Department Pioneer Memorial Museum

■ Veterans Hospital

CLEMENT   STREET

POINT LOBOS AVE

GEARY   BOULEVARD

ARGUELLO BLVD

Seal Rocks
■ Cliff House

25TH   AVENUE

RICHMOND

PARK PRESIDIO BOULEVARD

TURK   ST

MASONIC

University of San Francisco

M H de Young Memorial Museum

Conservatory of Flowers   Panhandle

Ocean Beach

□ FULTON   STREET

Golden Gate Park

Japanese Tea Garden

STANYAN STREET

HAIGHT
ASHBURY

Stow Lake

California Academy of Sciences

Strybing Arboretum & Botanical Gardens

LINCOLN WAY

PARNASSUS AVE

JUDAH   STREET

7TH   AVENUE

BUENA VISTA

GREAT   HIGHWAY

SUNSET   BOULEVARD

SUNSET

ORTEGA   STREET

19TH   AVENUE

Twin Peaks

FOREST HILL

Sunset Reservoir

TARAVAL   STREET

PARKSIDE

PORTOLA DRIVE

DIAMON
Gle

Pine Lake Park
SLOAT   ■ Sigmund Stern Grove

Mt Davidson
▲ 282m

San Francisco Zoological Gardens

BOULEVARD

ST FRANCIS WOOD

Stonestown Shopping Center

GLEN PARK

City College of San Francisco

Harding Park

LAKE MERCED BLVD

San Francisco State University

OCEAN   AVENUE

SOUTHERN   Freeway

Balb
Park

Lake Merced

Balb
Park

Golden Gate National Recreation Area

JOHN MUIR DRIVE

INGLESIDE

BROTHERHOOD   WAY

OCEAN VIEW

SKYLINE   BOULEVARD

280

San Francis

DALY CITY
● Daly City

A   B   C

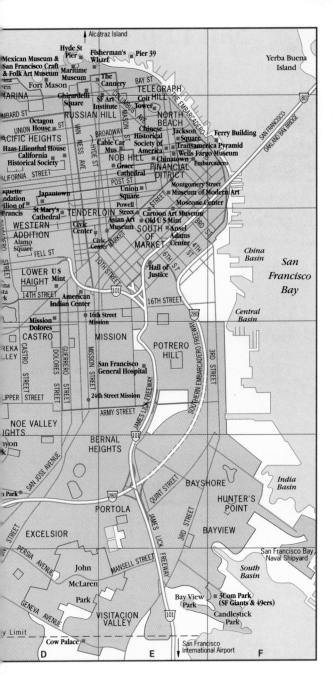

Alcatraz Island

Yerba Buena
Island

Mexican Museum &
San Francisco Craft
& Folk Art Museum

Hyde St
Pier

Fisherman's
Wharf

Pier 39

Maritime
Museum

The
Cannery

BAY ST

ina
en

Fort Mason

TELEGRAPH

80

SAN FRANCISCO

ARINA

Ghirardelli
Square

SF Art
Institute

Coit HILL
Tower

NORTH
BEACH

PACIFIC HEIGHTS

RUSSIAN HILL

COLUMBUS AVE

Chinese
Historical
Society of
America

Jackson
Square

Ferry Building

OAKLAND BAY BRIDGE

Octagon
House

UNION

ST

BROADWAY

Cable Car
Mus.

Transamerica Pyramid

Wells Fargo Museum

Haas-Lilienthal House
California
Historical Society

VAN NESS AVE

HYDE ST

MASON ST

NOB HILL

Chinatown

Embarcadero

ACIFIC HEIGHTS

ALIFORNIA STREET

Grace
Cathedral

FINANCIAL
DITRICT

POST ST

Montgomery Street

uquette
undation
vilion of
Francis

Japantown

Union
Square

Museum of Modern Art

St Mary's
Cathedral

Powell

Asian Art
Museum

Moscone Center

TENDERLOIN

Street

Cartoon Art Museum

WESTERN
ADDITION

Civic
Center

SOUTH
OF
MARKET

Old U S Mint

3RD ST

Ansel
Adams
Center

Alamo
Square

Civic Center

MARKET

4TH ST

China
Basin

ena
rk

FELL ST

10TH STREET

6TH ST

San
Francisco
Bay

LOWER
HAIGHT

US
Mint

Hall of
Justice

14TH STREET

American
Indian Center

16TH STREET

101

Central
Basin

16th Street
Mission

280

Mission
Dolores

CASTRO

MISSION

POTRERO
HILL

3RD STREET

EREKA
LEY

CASTRO STREET

DOLORES STREET

GUERRERO STREET

MISSION STREET

San Francisco
General Hospital

SOUTHERN EMBARCADERO FREEWAY

LIPPER STREET

24th Street Mission

ARMY STREET

NOE VALLEY
IGHTS

101

BERNAL
HEIGHTS

JAMES LICK FREEWAY

nyon
k

SAN JOSE AVENUE

280

QUINT STREET

BAYSHORE

India
Basin

n Park

PORTOLA

HUNTER'S
POINT

3RD STREET

STREET

EXCELSIOR

JAMES LICK FREEWAY

BAYVIEW

San Francisco Bay
Naval Shipyard

PERSIA AVENUE

John

MANSELL STREET

South
Basin

GENEVA AVENUE

McLaren

Park

Bay View
Park

3Com Park
(SF Giants & 49ers)

Candlestick
Park

y Limit

Cow Palace

VISITACION
VALLEY

101

San Francisco
International Airport

D

E

F

29

San Francisco

Its location on one of the world's largest natural harbours, the San Francisco Bay, provides this city with some fabulous natural views to backdrop the prevalent Victorian architecture. From hippie-haven Haight-Ashbury to the quaint Fisherman's Wharf, San Francisco has retained its historical charm.

Ironically, the horrible earthquakes for which this city is infamously known have created its most unusual feature: the hilly, twisting streets. Lombard Street, in swank Nob Hill, is 'the crookedest street in the world'.

Cable-cars make city travel fun as well as practical, with three main lines: Powell and Market streets from downtown to Fisherman's Wharf, and along California Street from Embarcadero to Van Ness. Tickets may be purchased on board the cars.

> '*It is an odd thing, but anyone who disappears is said to be seen in San Francisco.*'
>
> **OSCAR WILDE**
> while giving a lecture to the
> Bohemian Club, San Francisco
> (December 1882)

San Francisco

The Gold Rush of the mid-19th century brought a diverse ethnicity to San Francisco. Areas like Chinatown and Little Italy have preserved their different native cultures.

Out in the bay to the north is the infamous Alcatraz Island, the site of the notorious former prison. It is easily seen from Coit Tower, on top of Telegraph Hill. Russian Hill provides a panoramic look at the Golden Gate Bridge and the bay. To the north and east of the city lie the Napa Valley and Marin County, where wine-tasting is the hobby of choice.

Few places in the world can boast the sophistication of a major metropolitan area while also being offset by 42 hills and, and at the same time, surrounded by the serenity of lush vineyards as does San Francisco.

Famously crooked Lombard Street

What to See in San Francisco

ALCATRAZ ✪✪✪

Of the 14 islands punctuating the massive San Francisco Bay, 12-acre Alcatraz is the most famous. Rising 135 feet out of the bay, it is easy to see why it is nicknamed 'The Rock'. Although wild flowers are abundant on the island and the views of the bay and the Golden Gate bridge are breathtaking, most visitors visit the island to tour the

Alcatraz can be reached by a short ferry crossing from Fisherman's Wharf

✚ 29D6
☎ 415/705 5555
🕐 Hours vary, advance reservations recommended
🚢 Ferry from Pier 41, Fisherman's Wharf
👟 Moderate

massive fortress that covers most of the grounds. Built in 1858 as a military post, it soon became a military prison and finally a federal penitentiary.

Because of the severe tides and undertow of the surrounding chilly waters, escape from the prison was reputed to be impossible. Three inmates dug their way out of their prison cells and disappeared in 1962. No one knows if they made it to the mainland, but their bodies were never found. The prison closed soon after the attempt, and a group of Native Americans claimed the island as their birthright. Some of the buildings were burned before the National Park Service took control and reopened Alcatraz as a tourist attraction in 1973.

Three prominent movies have been filmed on the island: *Escape from Alcatraz*, *The Birdman of Alcatraz* and *The Rock*. Tours include a close-up look at the cells with audio-cassette narration by former prisoners and guards and exterior trail walks led by park rangers. Dress warmly and wear comfortable shoes.

ANSEL ADAMS CENTER FOR PHOTOGRAPHY ✪

Focusing on creative photography, both historical and contemporary, this centre is owned and operated by the Adams-founded 'Friends of Photography'. It features rotating exhibits of contemporary photography and a recently added photo-based, multi-media exhibit that is truly unique.

- 🕂 29E4
- ✉ 250 Fourth Street
- ☎ 415/495 7000
- 🕐 Tue–Sun 11–5, 1st Thu of month to 8
- ❓ Special and group tours
- ✋ Cheap

ASIAN ART MUSEUM ✪✪

More than 40 Asian countries are represented in this museum, the largest of its kind outside the Asian continent. Exclusive to this museum are works of Asian art spanning 4,000 years of Chinese history. It also houses outstanding exhibits from India, Japan and Korea and more than 300 works from the estates of Chinese emperors.

- 🕂 29E4
- ✉ Tea Garden Drive at Ninth Avenue, Golden Gate Park
- ☎ 414/379 8801
- 🕐 Wed–Sun 10–4:45
- ✋ Cheap, free 1st Wed of month (10–8:45)

Stone exhibit in the Asian Art Museum

CABLE CAR MUSEUM AND POWERHOUSE VIEWING GALLERY ✪✪

If you're fascinated by San Francisco's cable-cars, visit this working nerve centre and museum. On exhibit are the first cable-cars, which went unchanged for almost 100 years. Their design was modernised in 1982. Also housed in the three-level, red-brick 1907 barn are photographs, artefacts and a model collection. From the viewing gallery you can watch craftsmen working on the cars.

- 🕂 29E5
- ✉ 1201 Mason Street
- ☎ 415/474 1887
- 🕐 Daily 10–6
- ✋ Free

CALIFORNIA ACADEMY OF SCIENCES ✪✪✪

Dating back to the mid-19th century, this is considered one of the finest natural history museums in the world. The Morrison Planetarium has a 65-foot dome and a unique 5,000-pound star projector, built especially for the museum. Star shows are given daily. The Natural History Museum houses several galleries, an exhibit that allows visitors to 'experience' an earthquake, and a hands-on Discovery Room for children. The Steinhart Aquarium has almost 14,000 salt-water species which include octopuses, sea-horses, dolphins and sharks. The Wild California exhibit, with its incredible dioramas, is not to be missed. There is also a reproduction of a 300-year-old forest with life-like animals.

- 🕂 28C4
- ✉ Music Concourse, Golden Gate Park
- ☎ 415/750 7145
- 🕐 Daily 10–5
- ✋ Moderate; senior/children rates. Free 1st Wed of month

CALIFORNIA PALACE OF THE LEGION OF HONOR ✪✪✪

Refurbished in 1995, this classical palace was inspired by the Hotel de Salm in Paris, the site where Napoleon established the Legion D'Honneur. The Palace houses an extraordinary collection of 75,000 prints and drawings from the Achenbach Foundation, and expansive European art dating from 2500 BC through to the 20th century. Rodin's *The Thinker* is on display in the courtyard.

✝ 28A5
✉ 34th Avenue and Clement Street, Lincoln Park
☎ 415/750 3600
🕐 Tue–Sun 9:30–5:15, 1st Sat of month 9:30–8:45
🎫 Moderate; senior/children rates; free 2nd Wed of month

CARTOON ART MUSEUM ✪

This museum houses permanent and rotating exhibits of original two- and three-dimensional art and cartoon artefacts. You can see the original artwork and drawings used in the production of cartoons. Some exhibits go back to the 18th century. Video presentations are also part of the programme.

✝ 29E4
✉ 814 Mission Street
☎ 415/227 8666
🕐 Wed–Fri 11–5, Sat 10–5, Sun 1–5. Closed holidays
🎫 Cheap; senior/children rates

CHINESE HISTORICAL SOCIETY OF AMERICA ✪✪✪

The largest collection of Chinese-American artefacts in the US is housed here, including Chinese dragon heads, an 1880 Buddhist altar and a concise history of the Chinese experience in America, from 1840 to the present day.

✝ 29E5
✉ 650 Commercial Street
☎ 415/391 1188
🕐 Tue–Sat noon–4
🎫 Donation suggested

CIVIC CENTER PLAZA ✪✪

Dominated by the French Renaissance-inspired City Hall, the complex dates back to the 1906 earthquake. On the west end is the War Memorial and Performing Arts Center. The Center is home to the Louise M Davies Symphony Hall, the War Memorial Opera House and the War Memorial Veterans Building. The latter contains the San Francisco Museum of Modern Art and the Herbst Theatre, where the United Nations charter was signed in 1945. Other classically styled buildings in the plaza complex are the Civic Auditorium, the San Francisco Public Library and the State Building.

✝ 29D4
✉ Van Ness Avenue/Polk Street at Grove and McAllister streets
🕐 Interior closed until further notice due to seismic upgrading
🎫 Free

City Hall epitomises the Beaux-Arts style

A Walk Around Chinatown

This walk takes you through the largest Chinese community outside Asia.

Enter through the Chinatown Gate, at Bush Street and Grant Avenue.

Note the dragon-entwined lampposts and pagoda roofs as you are greeted by a cacophony of Chinese street merchants and the aromas of simmering noodles.

Walk north on Grant to the Dragon House Oriental Fine Arts and Antiques (No 455).

Continue up Grant to St Mary's Park where there's a 12-foot sculpture of Sun Yat-sen.

Continue north to Clay, turn right to Kearny, then left to Portsmouth Square. Across Kearny is the Holiday Inn.

Pop inside to the Chinese Cultural Center.

Go north on Kearny, to Pacific, then left to the New Asia restaurant (No 772).

This is a good choice for lunch.

Continue east on Pacific to Grant, then go left two blocks to Washington. Turn right.

Admire the three-tiered pagoda-style Bank of Canton, then continue west to the Tien Hou Temple (in Waverly Place on Washington). Around the corner is The Great China Herb Co (No 857), where sellers fill herbal prescriptions.

Continue west on Washington to Stockton, then turn left.

The Chinese Six Companies building (No 843) is an architectural wonder, with its curved roof tiles and elaborate cornices.

Walk south on Stockton to the Stockton Street Tunnel. A 15-minute walk through the tunnel brings you to downtown Union Square.

Distance
5 miles

Time
2–4 hours

Start point
Chinatown Gate
➕ 29E5

End point
Union Square
➕ 29E5

Lunch
New Asia (££)
✉ 772 Pacific Avenue
☎ 415/391 6666

Chinatown lion

➕ 29D6
✉ North of North Beach
🍴 Cafés, stands (£)
♿ Excellent

FISHERMAN'S WHARF ✪✪

Bustling Fisherman's Wharf is the centre of San Francisco's thriving tourist trade. It has many shops, street stands, food emporia and the like. Originally, it was an active base for San Francisco Bay's once busy fishing industry, until the late 1940s. A small fleet still operates.

➕ 28B5
✉ GGNRA, Building 201, Fort Mason, San Francisco, CA 94123
☎ 415/556 0560
🕐 Mon–Fri 8:30–4:30
🍴 Cafés, stands (£)
♿ Excellent
💷 Moderate

GOLDEN GATE NATIONAL ✪✪✪
RECREATION AREA

One of California's top attractions, this 1,000-acre expanse has museums, open-air performances and sporting events (▶ 19). Once an expanse of sand dunes, the area has been transformed into a botanical masterpiece.

The Strybing Arboretum and Botanical Gardens near the museum complex encompass 70 acres of plant life. The Japanese Tea Garden, with koi ponds and an 18th-century Buddha, is one of the most interesting spots in all San Francisco. The children's playground features a working carousel, and the park is host to dozens of cultural fairs and exhibits, and also food- and wine-tastings. In summer, there are operas and a popular Shakespearean festival.

The historical Fort Mason Center, once an embarkation point for American soldiers, houses a youth hostel, several theatres and four museums: the African-American Historical and Cultural Society, the Italian-American Museum, the Mexican Museum and the S S *Jeremiah O'Brien*. A Golden Gate Explorer Pass is reasonably priced and provides unlimited admission to all museums and gardens for six months.

The Japanese Tea Garden at Golden Gate Park

Did you know ?

For thousands of years, the only inhabitants near the current Golden Gate region were the Native American Ohlones, a sub-tribe of the Coast Miwok. Feasting mainly on oysters, they left huge piles of the shells which can still be seen. The largest pile is located at Coyote Hills, in southern Alameda County.

GRACE CATHEDRAL ✪✪

Taking over a half-century to build, this marvellous structure is a near-perfect replica of a Florentine cathedral. The singing of the Vespers each Thursday at 5:15PM is a truly spiritual experience.

- 29E5
- 1051 Taylor Street
- 415/776 6611
- Free, but donations accepted

HYDE STREET PIER AND HISTORICAL SHIPS ✪

In the Fisherman's Wharf area, this pier is the permanent home of several historical ships. Here you will find the ferry boat *Eureka* (1890), once the world's largest ferry boat, and the *Balclutha*, a square-rigged sailing ship from Scotland (1886), famed for rounding Cape Horn several times. Before leaving the area, drop into the National Maritime Museum at nearby Aquatic Park.

- 29D6
- 415/929 0202
- Summer, 10–6; autumn & winter, 10–5
- Cheap. National Park Golden Eagle Pass free

LOMBARD STREET ✪✪✪

Located in the Russian Hill district, this is San Francisco's famous 'crookedest' street. Traffic zigzags down it at 5mph, moving around colourful gardens which were established in the 1920s.

- 29D5
- Between Hyde and Leavenworth streets

MISSION SAN FRANCISCO DE ASIS (MISSION DOLORES) ✪✪✪

Founded in 1776 and moved to its present site in 1782, the mission is thought to be the oldest standing structure in the city. Adjoining is the Mission Dolores Basilica, the least changed of all California's existing missions. The architecture of Mission Dolores is a combination of Moorish, Mission and Corinthian styles, and the garden cemetery is filled with the burial sites of San Francisco pioneers.

- 29D4
- 316th and Dolores streets
- 415/621 8203
- Daily 9–4
- Donation requested

Stained glass at Mission Dolores, the sixth of 21 Missions founded by the Spanish in California

M H DE YOUNG MEMORIAL MUSEUM

An extensive collection of American artwork is contained in this 22-gallery complex set in Golden Gate Park. The museum's exhibits include paintings, sculpture, decorative arts, textiles and furniture. Some of the artwork dates to the mid-17th century. Also on display are classical and tribal works.

✚ 28C4
✉ Kennedy Drive and 8th Avenue, Golden Gate Park
☎ 415/750 3600
🕐 Wed–Sun 9:30–5:15
💲 Moderate. Free 1st Wed of month

NATURAL BRIDGES STATE BEACH 〇

Set in 65 acres, this beach, just before Santa Cruz, is a wonderful place to observe the migration of the colourful Monarch butterfly between mid-October and February. There are also tide pools to explore, as well as ecological and wildlife exhibits in the visitor centre.

✚ 68B3
✉ West Cliff Drive
☎ 408/423 4609
🕐 Beach daily 8–dusk; visitor centre 10–4
💲 Cheap

NORTH BEACH

This thriving, trendy neighbourhood, on the northeastern tip of San Francisco, is bound by Chinatown, the Financial District and Russian Hill. North Beach has a distinctly Italian atmosphere, and is central to most attractions, shops and restaurants in the area. Its heyday in the 1950s saw Jack Kerouac and other Beat Generation poets frequenting the cafés and bookstores, which remain important cultural meeting places. At the centre of the neighbourhood is **Coit Tower**, an impressive 210-foot landmark, built in 1934, reached on foot via the Filbert Steps by Darnell Place.

✚ 29E5

Coit Tower
☎ 415/362 0808
🕐 Daily 10–6

The Palace of Fine Arts, designed as a Roman ruin, incorporates a classical domed rotunda as its centre-piece

PALACE OF FINE ARTS

Home of the San Francisco International Film Festival, this Bernard Maybeck Greco-Romanesque rotunda is one of the most photographed buildings in San Francisco. Levelled by the great earthquake of 1906, it was completely rebuilt in 1915 and today presents continuing cultural events. Inside the complex is the Exploratorium, a wonderful hands-on science museum.

✚ 28C5
✉ 3601 Lyon Street
☎ 415/561 0360
🕐 Tue, Thu–Sun 10–5, Wed 10–9:30
💲 Moderate

ST MARY'S CATHEDRAL OF THE ASSUMPTION ✪✪✪

The radical architecture by Pietro Belluschi and Pier Luigi Nervi caused great debate during construction. Rising on concrete pylons to a height of 190 feet, the exterior resembles a washing machine agitator. Inside, however, the soaring cruciform is nothing short of breathtaking. The majestic pipe organ, itself, is worth seeing.

✚ 29D4
✉ 1111 Gough Street
☎ 415/567 2020
🕐 Mon–Fri 7–5, Sun 7–6:30
💲 Free, but donations accepted

SFMOMA: one of the finest museums of modern art in the country

SAN FRANCISCO MUSEUM OF MODERN ART ✪✪✪

This is the largest US museum devoted solely to modern art. Occupying a quarter-million square feet, it is the main structure in the new Yerba Buena Arts Center (SoMo district). Exhibits include a world-renowned collection of photography, and 20th-century works from such artists as Dali, O'Keefe and Jasper Johns. A current feature exhibit is 'From Matisse to Diebenkorn: Works from the Permanent Collection'.

✚ 29E5
✉ 151 Third Street
☎ 415/357 4000
🕐 Tue, Wed, Fri–Sun 11–6, Thu 11–9
💲 Moderate, senior/student rates, free 1st Tue of month

SAUSALITO ✪

This is the first small town in Marin County after crossing the Golden Gate Bridge. Once a fishing town, it has unfortunately been overrun with tacky tourist shops and no longer has the great charm of years past.

✚ 68B4
✉ 5 miles north of San Francisco
🚢 Ferry from Ferry Building or Fisherman's Wharf

TRANSAMERICA PYRAMID ✪✪

Depending on who you ask, this structure is either a landmark or an eyesore. Completed in 1972, the pyramid skyscraper juts 853 feet skyward, making it the tallest building in San Francisco.

✚ 29E5
✉ 600 Montgomery Street
🕐 Mon–Fri 8–4

Food & Drink

Because of its immensely diverse cultural make-up, California is a food lover's paradise. The major cities have authentic cuisine from almost every nation in the world.

Cuisine

Nearby Mexico exerts a strong influence, especially encouraging the generous use of avocados and salsa. There are taco stands everywhere. Cilantro is the spice of choice.

Sushi is fresh and popular. Chinese food, especially in San Francisco's Chinatown, is excellent. Fine dining establishments in the major cities feature delicious French cuisine.

All along the Coast are seafood houses to fit every budget. Fresh tuna and black cod are popular, while crab, oysters and jumbo shrimp cocktails satisfy lighter appetites.

Little Italy in San Francisco has the best

Below: *crab vendor on Fisherman's Wharf*
Right: *delicious seafood dishes are on offer all along the coast*

authentic Italian food, but pasta is the current food-fad of Californians and can be found everywhere. Beverly Hills has great Jewish delis and Solvang (Central Coast) features fine Scandinavian food.

Most visitors to the area, however, look forward to sampling genuine California cuisine. Menus are renowned for catering to swimsuit figures by being light, healthy and diet-friendly. For vegetarians, there is a huge year-round variety of locally grown vegetables (steamed), fresh salads with gourmet greens, and fresh fruits. Non-meat burgers and chicken are popular. The finest steaks can also be found, especially around the northern farming areas.

Lori's Diner – a popular venue

For a busy day of sightseeing, there are literally thousands of fast-food establishments. Even most of the small, inland towns have the major chains. In-N-Out Burger is a good choice for those on the run.

Beverages

Health-conscious Californians consume more bottled water per capita than any other state in the US. This may be due to the fact that a large part of the state has a desert-like climate and bottled water is easy to carry. Restaurants and markets offer a wide selection of both carbonated and uncarbonated types. Especially in the Palm Springs area, there are many roadside stands offering tasty 'date shakes'.

Star Gazing
When dining and drinking in LA, remember that 'star-gazing' may not necessarily be an exercise in astronomy. You could find yourself rubbing elbows with a celebrity straight off the screen as you satisfy your appetite. There is year-round patio dining, and casual attire is the norm. Most establishments accept all major credit cards.

Californian wines are in a class of their own

Although there are a few local breweries, imported beers seem to be favoured by the locals, so you can find almost any of the popular brands. Mexico's Corona is a top choice. Micro-breweries are rapidly gaining popularity, so check out some of the local beer-bistros for thirst-quenching treats.

German Jagermeister is the fad liquor of the hip who haunt the Sunset Strip, but the Mexican margarita is a time-tested standard. The martini is said to have originated in San Francisco.

Wine is said to appease and to have dietary and health considerations. Because so much excellent wine is produced in the state, the selection is overwhelming and costs are relatively affordable. Wineries of great renown include Mondavi, Beringer, Domaine Chandon, Louis M Martini, Buena Vista, Sebastiani and Korbel Champagne. A favourite is Mondavi's unfiltered Cabernet Sauvignon, and 'blush' fad wines are also popular these days. Try Sutter Home's 'White Zinfandel', a popular, inexpensive and refreshing brand, perfect for summer sipping.

UNION STREET ✪✪✪

29D5

Octagon House
✉ 2645 Gough Street
☎ 415/441 7512
🕐 2nd and 4th Thu and 2nd Sun of each month (except Jan), noon–3. Closed holidays
💰 Contributions

Union Street runs east–west from Battery Street in North Beach to the Presidio. It is one of the city's most fashionable areas in which to live and shop, and with its many beautifully restored Victorian mansions that have been converted into boutiques, art galleries and cafés, it is a must-see. Scattered among the bustling retail spots are several landmarks that should not be missed. The **Octagon House** is a pale-blue, eight-sided structure that features antique furniture from the 18th and 19th centuries. Also of interest is an exhibit containing the signatures of 54 of the 56 original signatories of the Declaration of Independence.

UNIVERSITY OF CALIFORNIA AT SANTA CRUZ ✪

68B3
✉ Bay and High Street
☎ 408/459 4008
🕐 Student-led tours Mon–Fri 10:30 & 1:30
💰 Free, parking cheap

On the campus are the remains of several buildings from the Cowell Ranch, dating back to the mid-19th century. Other outstanding buildings include two art galleries and the Long Marine Aquarium. The most popular exhibit in the aquarium is a virtually flawless skeleton of a blue whale. Eight colleges make up this 2,000-acre site, overlooking Monterey Bay and Santa Cruz.

WELLS FARGO HISTORY MUSEUM ✪✪

29E5
✉ 420 Montgomery Street
☎ 415/396 2619
🕐 Mon–Fri 9–5. Closed bank holidays
💰 Free

Located in the Wells Fargo Bank Building, the museum contains artefacts from the Old West and the California Gold Rush, and records the rise and fall of the company. There is a superbly preserved stagecoach and other interesting pieces from early years to the present.

A Drive Through Marin County

This drive takes you through scenic Marin County.

Begin at the Presidio in north San Francisco. Cross the Golden Gate Bridge and continue north on Highway 101.

Sausalito (➤ 39) is to your left.

Proceed north to the Tamalpais Valley exit and follow the signs to Muir Woods National Monument.

Here you can enjoy the beauty of the redwoods.

A dramatic panorama unfolds from the summit of Mount Tamalpais

Return to the 101 and continue northward.

Stop at the Marin County Civic Center, an architectural masterpiece designed by Frank Lloyd Wright in 1957.

Backtrack along the 101, through San Rafael, to Highway 580. Follow it across the Richmond–San Rafael Bridge.

Right before the bridge is San Quentin Prison. As you cross the bridge, San Francisco Bay is on your right and San Pablo Bay on your left.

A short distance past the bridge, take the 80 Freeway south to Berkeley.

Sites to see on the University of Berkeley campus include the Botanical Garden, Lawrence Hall of Science and the Phoebe Apperson Hearst Museum of Anthropology.

Continuing back on the 80 southbound, follow the highway past Emeryville and across the San Francisco–Oakland Bay Bridge.

Look right to see Treasure Island Naval Station and Alcatraz (➤ 32).

Take the first exit off the bridge to Fisherman's Wharf.

Distance
120 miles

Time
6–8 hours, depending on time spent at attractions

Start point
The Presidio
 28C5

End point
Fisherman's Wharf
✚ 29D6

Lunch
San Rafael–Panama Hotel and Restaurant (££)
✉ 4 Bay View Street
☎ 415/457 3993
🕐 daily 11:30–2:30 and 5:30–9:30 (closed for dinner on Monday)

43

Los Angeles

Whether you come for the beaches, mountains, museums or movie stars, Los Angeles teems with activity. Bring your sunglasses and your tanning lotion because here in California there is plenty of sunshine. For dedicated sun-seekers, beautiful beaches stretch along the western edge of this seemingly endless metropolis. Zuma Beach is one of the best for enjoying the pastime made famous by the music of The Beach Boys – surfing.

At Venice Beach you can either stroll barefoot along the beach or join the hustle along the Boardwalk, where vendors hawk their souvenirs. This is home to some of the nation's most colourful characters: musicians, magicians and mime artists, as well as Muscle Beach body builders.

'Call Los Angeles any dirty name you like – Six Suburbs in Search of a City, Paradise with a Lobotomy, anything – but the fact remains that you are already living in it before you get there.'

AUSTRALIAN CRITIC
CLIVE JAMES,
London Observer (1979)

———————•———————

A distinctive LA landmark, the folk art extravaganza of Watts Towers

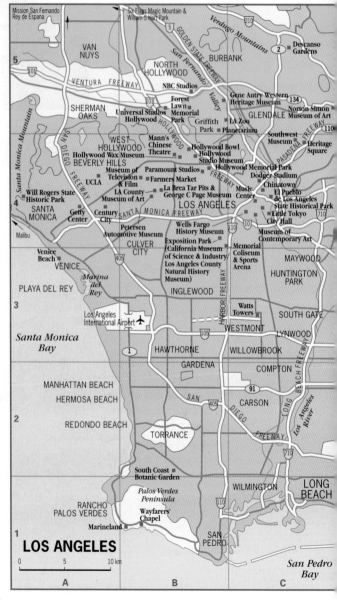

Mission San Fernando
Rey de Espana

Six Flags Magic Mountain &
William S Hart Park

Verdugo Mountains

VAN
NUYS

NORTH
HOLLYWOOD

BURBANK

Descanso
Gardens

San Fernando Valley

GOLDEN STATE FREEWAY

VENTURA FREEWAY

SHERMAN
OAKS

NBC Studios

Forest
Lawn
Memorial
Park

Gene Autry Western
Heritage Museum

GLENDALE

Norton Simon
Museum of Art

Universal Studios
Hollywood

Griffith
Park

LA Zoo
Planetarium

Southwest
Museum

Heritage
Square

WEST
HOLLYWOOD

Mann's
Chinese
Theatre

Hollywood Bowl
Hollywood
Studio Museum

BEVERLY HILLS

Hollywood Wax Museum

Hollywood Memorial Park

Museum of
Television
& Film

Paramount Studios

Dodger Stadium

Chinatown

UCLA

Farmers Market

Music
Center

El Pueblo
de Los Angeles
State Historical Park

La Brea Tar Pits &
George C Page Museum

LA County
Museum of Art

LOS ANGELES

Little Tokyo
City Hall

Will Rogers State
Historic Park

SANTA
MONICA

Getty
Center

Century
City

SANTA MONICA FREEWAY

Museum of
Contemporary Art

Malibu

Petersen
Automotive Museum

Wells Fargo
History Museum

MAYWOOD

Venice
Beach

CULVER
CITY

Exposition Park
(California Museum
of Science & Industry
Los Angeles County
Natural History
Museum)

Memorial
Coliseum
& Sports
Arena

HUNTINGTON
PARK

VENICE

Marina
del
Rey

PLAYA DEL REY

INGLEWOOD

SOUTH GATE

Santa Monica
Bay

Los Angeles
International Airport

HARBOR FREEWAY

Watts
Towers

HAWTHORNE

WESTMONT

LYNWOOD

LONG BEACH FREEWAY

WILLOWBROOK

GARDENA

COMPTON

MANHATTAN BEACH

HERMOSA BEACH

SAN

CARSON

Los Angeles River

REDONDO BEACH

DIEGO

FREEWAY

TORRANCE

South Coast
Botanic Garden

WILMINGTON

LONG
BEACH

Palos Verdes
Peninsula

RANCHO
PALOS VERDES

Wayfarers'
Chapel

Marineland

SAN
PEDRO

LOS ANGELES

0   5   10 km

San Pedro
Bay

A   B   C

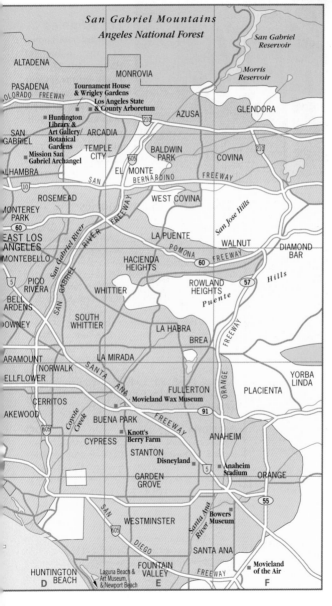

San Gabriel Mountains
Angeles National Forest

San Gabriel
Reservoir

ALTADENA
MONROVIA

Morris
Reservoir

PASADENA
COLORADO FREEWAY
Tournament House
& Wrigley Gardens
Los Angeles State
& County Arboretum
GLENDORA

AZUSA

■ Huntington
Library &
Art Gallery/
Botanical
Gardens
ARCADIA

SAN
GABRIEL
TEMPLE
CITY
BALDWIN
PARK
COVINA

■ Mission San
Gabriel Archangel
EL MONTE

ALHAMBRA
BERNARDINO
FREEWAY

ROSEMEAD
WEST COVINA

MONTEREY
PARK
San Jose Hills

EAST LOS
ANGELES
LA PUENTE
POMONA
WALNUT
DIAMOND
BAR

MONTEBELLO
60 FREEWAY

PICO
RIVERA
HACIENDA
HEIGHTS
57
Hills

BELL
GARDENS
WHITTIER
ROWLAND
HEIGHTS
Puente

DOWNEY
SOUTH
WHITTIER
LA HABRA

BREA

PARAMOUNT
LA MIRADA

NORWALK
SANTA

BELLFLOWER
YORBA
LINDA

CERRITOS
FULLERTON
PLACENTIA

LAKEWOOD
Movieland Wax Museum
91

BUENA PARK
FREEWAY

CYPRESS
Knott's
Berry Farm
ANAHEIM

STANTON
Disneyland
5
■ Anaheim
Stadium
ORANGE

GARDEN
GROVE
55

WESTMINSTER
Bowers
Museum

SANTA ANA

HUNTINGTON
BEACH
Laguna Beach &
Art Museum,
& Newport Beach
FOUNTAIN
VALLEY
FREEWAY
■ Movieland
of the Air

D
E
F

47

Los Angeles

Probably best known as the home of Hollywood, LA is a haven for the famous and those who never quite made it. Buy a map and take a self-guided driving tour past the homes of some of Hollywood's most famous residents.

One of Hollywood's landmark hotels

 46A4

✉ Visitors Bureau, 239 S Bundy Drive, Beverly Hills 90212

☎ 310/248 1015

What to See in Los Angeles

BEVERLY HILLS ✪✪✪

The City of Stars is the place where shopping and the entertainment industry each vie for their place as the number one attraction (▶ 49). Here you will find some of the most expensive real estate in the country. The city's most recognisable zip code (90210) receives over 14 million visitors a year, making it the most popular destination in Los Angeles.

Beverly Hills has several main thoroughfares, all running east to west. Sunset Boulevard, at the north end, roughly splits the commercial and residential areas. Wilshire Boulevard is the main thoroughfare to the business and commercial centres. At the south end, Pico Boulevard marks the Beverly Hills border. This incorporated city has its own police and fire departments and its own library, complete with gold-coloured library cards.

✚ 46C4

✉ 900 block of Broadway

CHINATOWN ✪✪

The cultural centre of this unique community is home to about 5 per cent of LA's 200,000 Chinese residents. Chinatown encompasses 16 square blocks, and its downtown area is filled with Asian architecture, good restaurants and import shops. The Kong Chow Temple is exquisite.

✚ 46C4

✉ 200 N Spring Street

☎ 213/485 2891

🕐 Mon–Fri 9–4

✋ Free

CITY HALL ✪

This building was the first skyscraper to be built in Los Angeles and served as The Daily Planet Building in the *Superman* television series of the 1950s. Guided tours are free and last 45 minutes. There is an observation deck on the 27th floor.

A Walk Around Beverly Hills

This walk begins on one of the most expensive shopping streets in the world.

Walk north from Wilshire on Rodeo Drive.

Do a spot of window-shopping in Tiffany's, Saks and Gucci (➤ 107).

Proceed north several blocks to Little Santa Monica, then go east (right) a couple of blocks to Crescent.

On the corner of Crescent you'll see the historic former Beverly Hills Post Office and the magnificent Beverly Hills Municipal Building. The latter houses City Hall and the Beverly Hills library and police station.

Take a left on Crescent and proceed north across Santa Monica Boulevard and through the Beverly Hills 'flatlands'.

The homes along here are absolutely gorgeous.

At Sunset Boulevard, walk across to the newly restored Beverly Hills Hotel (➤ 101).

Take a few minutes to stroll through the splendid lobby.

Proceed east on Sunset to the West Hollywood business district.

Here you will pass the famous Roxy theatre, Spago restaurant and The Whiskey A Go-Go.

Continue east, stopping for lunch at the chic Sunset Plaza, then on to Sunset. Turn right on Crescent Heights Road and go south to Melrose Avenue. Turn left on to Melrose and walk several blocks to Fairfax Avenue.

At this corner is the sprawling CBS Television City. Tours are available, as well as free tickets to live tapings of television shows.

South of CBS is the Farmers' Market, where your tour ends.

Distance
4 miles

Time
3–4 hours, depending on time spent at attractions

Start point
Beverly Hills, corner of Wilshire and Rodeo
46A4

End point
Farmers' Market
46A4

Lunch
Chin Chin (£)
✉ 8618 Sunset Boulevard
☎ 310/652 1818

Farmers' Market is a mix of fruit and vegetable stalls, souvenir shops and food stands

49

A street market in El Pueblo State Historic Park

🚩 46C5
✉ 1418 Descanso Drive, La
Cañada Flintridge
☎ 818/952 4400
🕐 Daily 9–4:30. Closed
Christmas Day
💵 Cheap, special discounts,
free 3rd Tue of month

🚩 46C4
✉ Betweeen Alameda,
Arcadia, Spring and Macy
streets
☎ 213/628 1274
🕐 Mon–Sat 10–3. Closed
holidays
💵 Free

🚩 46B4

**California Museum of
Science and Industry**
✉ Exposition Boulevard at
Figueroa
☎ 213/744 7400
🕐 Daily 10–5
💵 Free, small charge for
IMAX

**California Afro-American
Museum**
☎ 213/744 7432
🕐 Tue–Sun 10–5
💵 Cheap

**LA County Museum of
Natural History**
☎ 213/744 3414
🕐 Tue–Sun 10–5
💵 Cheap, free first Tue of
month

DESCANSO GARDENS ⬤⬤

These glorious gardens cover 65 acres, including a 30-acre California live oak forest. Over 100,000 camellias collected from around the world flourish here, as do many roses, lilacs and other blossoms. The Japanese Garden has a serene teahouse. It is worth the short drive north of the city.

EL PUEBLO DE LOS ANGELES STATE ⬤⬤
HISTORICAL PARK

Here, on 44 acres near downtown, you can visit the Avila Adobe (the oldest adobe house), Masonic Hall, Old Plaza Church and Sepulveda House. Founded in 1781, the main attraction for most visitors is Olvera Street, an open-air Mexican-style market place lined with speciality shops, vendors, cafés and restaurants.

EXPOSITION PARK ⬤⬤⬤

The Los Angeles Memorial Coliseum was host to the Olympics in 1932 and 1984. Several museums are contained within, including the **California Museum of Science and Industry**, with interactive exhibits, Aerospace Complex and the surround-vision IMAX theatre, featuring a five-storey-high screen. Other museums include the **California Afro-American** and the **Los Angeles County Museum of Natural History,** with three floors of dinosaur, fossil and cultural exhibits.

> ### *Did you know ?*
>
> *Comedian Robin Williams said of Hollywood,
> 'Living in Hollywood is like being in high school –
> only with money.'*

FOREST LAWN MEMORIAL PARK ✪✪

A cemetery may seem like an unusual attraction, but there are 300 lush acres of grounds here, with reproductions of such works as da Vinci's *Last Supper*, and the world's largest religious painting on canvas, Jan Styke's *The Crucifixion*. Also not to be missed are the ornate tombstones of celebrities and the beautiful gardens. Forest Lawn cemetery is the final resting place of such Hollywood film legends as Humphrey Bogart, Errol Flynn, Spencer Tracy, Stan Laurel, Carole Lombard, W C Fields, Jean Harlow and Cary Grant.

✝ 46B5
✉ 1712 South Glendale Avenue, Glendale
☎ 818/241 4151
🕐 Daily 8–5
✋ Free

Statue in Forest Lawn Memorial Park

THE GETTY CENTER ✪✪✪

Opened in December 1997, this billion-dollar arts complex sits high on a hill off the 405 San Diego freeway to the north of the city. Although still in its infancy it seems destined to become one of LA's main attractions. With everything from Greek sculptures to paintings by European masters and modern photography, the museum is surrounded by ponds, beautiful landscaping and a fine herb garden.

✝ 46A4
Getty Center
✉ 1200 Getty Center Drive
☎ 310/440 7300
🕐 Tue–Sun 10–5
✋ Free ($5 fee for parking)

GRIFFITH PARK ✪✪✪

Here, in the Santa Monica Mountain range, Griffith Park contains the LA Zoo, Griffith Observatory and Planetarium, as well as Travel Town, an outdoor transportation museum. The Observatory is the perfect spot to view the Hollywood sign and the entire city, while the Planetarium features incredible laserium shows. There are horseback riding and children's rides and attractions, plus plenty of picnic areas.

✝ 46B5
✉ Mount Hollywood
☎ 213/664 1191 (Observatory/Planetarium); 213/666 4090 (Zoo)
🕐 Hours vary so call for information
✋ The park is free; some attractions have moderate fees

HOLLYWOOD (► 21, TOP TEN)

HOLLYWOOD WAX MUSEUM ✪✪

Over 220 of Hollywood's greatest stars, political leaders and sports greats – all made of wax, but very lifelike – are on show at the Hollywood Wax Museum. Also included are displays on television, motion pictures and religion. Exhibits rotate every six months or so. The Chamber of Horrors is a favourite, as well as the recent additions of current stars.

✝ 46B4
✉ 6767 Hollywood Boulevard
☎ 323/462 8860
🕐 Sun–Thu 10–midnight, Fri–Sat to 2AM
✋ Moderate

51

47D5
1151 Oxford Road, San Marino
626/405 2141
Tue–Fri 12–4:30pm, Sat–Sun 10:30–4:30
Moderate

HUNTINGTON LIBRARY, ART GALLERY AND BOTANICAL GARDENS ✪✪✪

The historical library contains over four million items, including art treasures and an extraordinary treasury of rare and precious manuscripts. After taking in the Huntington's art and books, take a walk through the immaculate botanical gardens, the best in the state. Here, 15 separate garden areas contain around 14,000 different types of plants and trees. Arrive early because the grounds fill up fast.

46C4
First Street & Central Avenue

LITTLE TOKYO ✪✪

The city's Japanese quarter features the 40-shop Japanese Village Plaza, which resembles a rural village. Also here are Noguchi Plaza, with its fan-shaped Japan America Theatre, the Japanese American National Museum, and quiet Japanese gardens. Some great sushi bars can also be found here.

46C1
Pier J, Long Beach Harbor
310/435 3511
Daily 10–6
Free; moderate-priced guided tours

LONG BEACH ✪✪

This rapidly growing city, just south of Los Angeles, is now California's fifth largest city. Its Shoreline Village and Wilmore Park surround the Convention and Entertainment Center, a popular corporate convention spot. Boats to Catalina Island depart from Golden Shore Boulevard.

Of special interest is the *Queen Mary*, which came to rest in Long Beach in 1967. With 12 decks and weighing in at 50,000 tons, it is the largest passenger ship ever built, the *crème de la crème* of 1932 art deco luxury. There are lots of shops and eateries on board.

47D5
301 N Baldwin Avenue, Arcadia
818/821 3222
Daily 9–4
Cheap; various discounts

LOS ANGELES STATE AND COUNTY ARBORETUM ✪✪✪

The trees and shrubs in the 127-acre splendour of the Los Angeles Arboretum are arranged according to the

The delightful Queen Anne guest house in Los Angeles Arboretum

continent they originate from. Also featured are green-houses, a bird sanctuary and historic buildings like the Queen Anne Cottage, home of the estate's former owner, Elia Jackson Baldwin. Picnic areas and tours available.

The cutting edge of contemporary sculpture on display at MOCA

MANN'S CHINESE THEATRE ✪✪✪
Originally Grauman's Chinese Theatre, Mann's, a prime Hollywood tourist attraction, is a good starting point for a tour of Los Angeles (➤ 21). The theatre was opened in 1927 by showman Sid Grauman, and whenever a film was premiered here, stars left their hand or foot prints.

✚ 46B4
✉ 6925 Hollywood Boulevard
☎ 323/464 8111

MUSEUM OF CONTEMPORARY ART (MOCA) ✪✪✪
This seven-tiered museum (much of which is below street level) has eleven giant pyramidal skylights and a 53-foot barrel-vaulted entrance. It is dedicated to works of art since the 1940s and regularly features travelling exhibitions.

✚ 46B4
✉ 250 S Grand Avenue
☎ 213/621 2766
🕐 Tue, Wed, Fri–Sun 11–5, Thu to 8
♿ Moderate, free Thu 5–8

PETERSEN AUTOMOTIVE MUSEUM ✪✪✪
If you are an automotive fan, the Petersen Museum, with one of the largest auto collections in the world, is a must. It explores automotive history and culture from the earliest jalopies. Highlights are the 1957 Ferrari 250 Testa Rossa, and customised cars from Dean Jeffries and George Barris.

✚ 46B4
✉ 6060 Wilshire Boulevard
☎ 213/930 CARS
🕐 Sat–Thu 10–6, Fri to 9
♿ Moderate

SOUTHWEST MUSEUM ✪
This mission-style building, high above downtown LA, focuses on Native American art, including jewellery, basketwork and weaving. The museum's founder, Charles Lummis, director of the Los Angeles Library in 1907, also donated rare books to the museum.

✚ 46C4
✉ 234 Museum Drive
☎ 213/221 2163
🕐 Tue–Sat 11–5, Sun 1–5
♿ Moderate

UNIVERSAL STUDIOS AND CITYWALK ✪✪✪

For a fascinating behind-the-scenes look at movie-making, plan to spend the better part of a day at Universal Studios, the world's biggest and busiest motion picture and television studio-cum-theme park. Citywalk features outdoor dining and a wide variety of shops that are a cut above what you might expect. There are huge outdoor screens that show music videos and movie previews and a theatre complex shows all the latest movies.

The upper and lower sections are connected by a long escalator, making the immense 420-acre park easy to navigate. Some of the more interesting sets still standing are from such films as *The Sting, Animal House* and *Home Alone*. There are theme rides based on other successful films such as *Batman* and *Jurassic Park*.

➕ 46B5
✉ 100 Universal City Plaza, Universal City
☎ 818/508 9600
🕐 Mon–Fri 9–7; weekends 9:30–7 year-round
✋ Expensive

The beachfront, Venice Beach – haunt of skateboarders and rollerbladers

VENICE BEACH ✪✪

Just south along the beach from Santa Monica is Venice Beach. Although it appears to be a throwback to the 1960s, it is really a thriving enclave for modern bohemians. The neighbourhood was founded in 1905 by Abbot Kinney, who hoped to create a haven for artistic types. Gondolas were imported from Italy and, for a time, the canals were eerily similar to those in Europe. Try a free self-guided tour. The most popular today is the Ocean Front Walk, teeming with visitors, street performers and souvenir stands. You can also rent a bicycle or rollerblades.

➕ 46A3
✉ 15 miles from downtown Los Angeles, access via Lincoln Boulevard

Kinney's Venice of America
☎ 310/827 2366 (local history of the Venice area, artefacts and vintage photographs)

WATTS TOWERS ✪✪✪

Italian immigrant Simon Rodia took 30 years to build these extraordinary towers by himself, using scraps of whatever materials he could find. Saved from demolition by local residents, the towers are currently being restored.

➕ 46C3
✉ 1765 E 107th Street
❓ Closed while renovation is carried out

A Drive Around Los Angeles

This drive winds through some of LA's most exclusive neighbourhoods, then west to Malibu.

From the Hollywood Bowl, drive north, veering to the left on to Cahuenga Boulevard. Drive to the Mulholland Drive turn-off, go left and continue on to Mulholland west.

Along Mulholland are several turn-offs for viewing the city and the San Fernando Valley below.

Continue westward on Mulholland to the 405 Freeway, entering southbound.

Take the first exit (Getty Center Drive), the site of the new Getty Center (➤ 51).

Continue south on the 405 to Sunset Boulevard and exit. Turn right on to Sunset and drive westward. Continue to Bundy Drive and turn left at the light. Travel east about a mile to reach the stoplight at San Vincente. Go through the light, turn left and right to continue on Bundy.

Just past the next stop-light is the Simpson-Goldman murder scene, to your right.

Return to Sunset and turn left. Travel west on Sunset through the Pacific Palisades, to Pacific Coast Highway, along the ocean.

At the junction of Sunset and the Pacific Coast Highway is Gladstones 4 Fish, a great place to take lunch.

Continue north on Pacific Coast Highway to Malibu. Las Tunas State Beach is a good beach to spend time on. Continue north to Malibu Canyon Road and turn right at the light. Follow the road over the Santa Monica Mountains and turn into Las Virgines Road. Continue to the on-ramp to the 101 Freeway, and follow it south to the Highland exit and the Hollywood Bowl.

Distance
60 miles

Time
About 5 hours

Start/end point
Hollywood Bowl
✚ 46B4

Lunch
Gladstones 4 Fish (££)
✉ 17300 Pacific Coast Highway, Pacific Palisades
☎ 310/454 3474

Hollywood landmark: entrance to Paramount Studios

San Diego

The beautiful Mission Bay and world-famous San Diego Zoo are highlights of this city, one of the most liveable areas in the US.

For excitement, there's Sea World or the San Diego Wild Animal Park. For serenity, the Japanese Friendship Garden's traditional sand-and-stone garden and wooded canyon view is the perfect picnic spot. Those interested in science will appreciate The Reuben H Fleet Space Theater and Science Center. Its Space Theater's OMNIMAX films bring outer space up close, while the Aerospace Museum showcases heroes of aviation and space.

Old Town commemorates the first permanent settlement in California and still has many of the city's original buildings. Trolley tours through the six-block area make seeing the sights easy.

> ‘ *Wouldn't it be wonderful*
> *to have a zoo in San Diego?*
> *I believe I'll build one.* ’

> DR HENRY WEGEFORTH,
> on hearing the roar of caged lions at
> the California Panama
> Exposition (1906)

The modern San Diego skyline

San Diego

San Diego rarely gets rain, never freezes, has an average annual daytime temperature between 58 and 70°F, and over 70 miles of superb sandy beaches. California's second largest city, it retains a small-town ambience. Ralph Waldo Emerson must have visited San Diego when he said 'California has better days and more of them.'

The lighthouse at Cabrillo National Monument

What to See in San Diego

BALBOA PARK (▶ 16, TOP TEN)

➕ 59A2

THE BEACHES   ✪✪✪

The most popular of the city's beaches is Pacific Beach (known as 'PB' by the locals), which features The Tourmaline Surfing Park, a surfer's paradise. Mission Beach has a three-mile walk of shops and skateboard, rollerblade and bicycle rental stands. Ocean Beach is one of the liveliest in San Diego, and a good place to fish. Point Loma is an upscale beach, with spectacular views of the naval ships' comings and goings.

CABRILLO NATIONAL MONUMENT   ✪✪

➕ 59A1
✉ 10 miles west of I-8 on Catalina Boulevard
☎ 619/557 5450
🕐 Daily 9–5:15
🎫 Cheap

A 144-acre park along steep cliffs, Cabrillo rewards with great views of San Diego Bay, and it's an especially good place to spot gray whales migrating to Mexico between mid-December and mid-March. The Old Point Loma Lighthouse, dating from 1855, is 25 miles out to sea, but visible from here on a clear day.

CORONADO ISLAND   ✪✪✪

➕ 59B1
✉ Visitor Center at 1111 Orange Avenue
☎ 619/236 1212

A combination of wealthy enclave and naval base, Coronado sits just across the bay from downtown San Diego. The easiest way to reach it is on the Bay Ferry. Leaving from Broadway Pier downtown, the ferry arrives

at Old Ferry Landing in Coronado in 15 minutes. You can also reach the island via the towering San Diego–Coronado Bay Bridge (toll). The main attraction on the island is Hotel Del Coronado (► 102). A testament to the beauty of Victorian architecture, the 'Del' was opened in 1888, and film buffs might remember it as one of the main locations in Marilyn Monroe's film *Some Like It Hot*.

☎ 619/437 8788 (Visitor Centre), 619/234 4111 (Bay Ferry information)
🎟 Cheap

The Victorian-style Hotel del Coronado

59B1
Balboa Park
619/234 0739
Sun, 1st Tue of month
Free

59A3
10 miles north of San Diego via I 805 or Highway 1

GASLAMP QUARTER (➤ 62) ✪✪

HOUSE OF PACIFIC RELATIONS ✪✪

The culture and art of 31 nations is housed in the museum's 15 California/Spanish-style cottages located in the Pan American Plaza. Other Plaza attractions are the Aerospace Museum, San Diego Automotive Museum and the open-air Starlight Bowl.

LA JOLLA ✪✪✪

Pronounced *La Hoya* (Spanish for 'The Jewel') this picturesque cove must surely be one of the prettiest places in the whole state. Just north of San Diego proper, it is considered the best place to examine marine life in a wild environment. This unspoiled piece of coastline offers expensive restaurants and boutiques on its two main thoroughfares: Prospect Street and Girard Avenue. Just north of La Jolla are the equally scenic towns of Del Mar and Solana Beach. Relatively undiscovered by tourists, these beaches epitomise the beauty and tranquillity of Southern California.

The crystal clear waters at La Jolla

59B1
1306 North Harbor Drive
619/234 9153
Daily 9–8
Moderate

MARITIME MUSEUM OF SAN DIEGO ✪✪✪

Basically just three ships are moored on the Embarcadero but oh, what legendary ships they are! The pick of the bunch is the 1863 *Star of India*, a fully equipped three-mast sailing ship, the oldest iron-hulled ship in America still afloat. San Francisco's *Berkeley* was the ferry used to evacuate victims of the 1906 earthquake. The 1904 steam-powered yacht *Medea* still occasionally sails around the Bay.

Mission San Diego de Alcala was Serra's first mission in California

> ### *Did you know ?*
>
> The California Tower carillon has no bells,
> but rather hammers bang against separate metal strips
> slightly larger than coat hangers.

MISSION BAY PARK ✪✪

There are miles of cycling paths throughout this huge aquatic park, and a bicycle rental stand can be found just off East Mission Bay Drive. Kite flying and volleyball are popular pastimes here, and just about anything to do with the water, as well as golf, picnicking and camping, can be found. The park is also the home of Sea World (➤ 64), and for many families the main reason for coming here. Just next to the park is Fiesta Island, popular with the locals for jet skiing and the curious game of 'over the line' baseball.

✚ 59A2
✉ 2688 E Mission Bay Drive
☎ 619/276 8200
🕐 Daily
🎟 Free

MUSEUM OF MAN ✪✪

This museum, located below the California Tower, offers eclectic, ever-changing exhibits from Californians and Hopi tribes, ancient Egypt and mummies, to Mayas and early man (➤ 16).

✚ 59B1
✉ Balboa Park
☎ 619/239 2001
🕐 Daily 10–4:30
🎟 Cheap

OLD TOWN SAN DIEGO STATE HISTORICAL PARK ✪✪✪

The remains of the first European settlement in California, Old Town is preserved with National Park status. The most important area of Old Town is the Mission San Diego de Alcala, California's first mission, founded in 1769 by Father Junipero Serra. Restored and still used for services, it has beautiful gardens and adobe structures and houses the Museum de Luis Jayme. One of the oldest buildings, Casa de Estudillo, has survived several hundred years.

Old Town Plaza was a general meeting place and centre for festivals, religious celebrations and even bullfights in the mid-1800s. Here you'll find the visitors' centre where you can sign up for free tours of the grounds.

✚ 59B2
✉ 10818 San Diego Mission Road
☎ 619/281 8449
🕐 Daily 9–5, closed Jan 1, Thanksgiving, Christmas Day
🎟 Moderate. Cheap, senior rates for Mission

A Walk Around San Diego

Distance
3½ miles

Time
3 hours

Start point
Visitors' Center, Old Town
State Historic Park
✚ 59B2

End point
Old Town Plaza
✚ 59B2

Lunch
Casa de Bandini (£)
✉ 2754 Calhoun Street
☎ 619/297 8211
🕐 Daily 11–9:30

Starting at the Old Town visitors' centre, you pass historic buildings, museums and sites that encompass the oldest and most beautiful part of San Diego.

From the visitors' centre, walk southward and turn east on San Diego Avenue, continuing to the Machado–Silvas Adobe house.

This is one of the more famous buildings built in the mid-19th century, and houses the Courthouse and the Colorado House/Wells Fargo Museum.

After touring the house, continue a short distance north to Mason Street.

Here you will see the Mason Street School. Built in 1865, this one-room building was San Diego's first publicly owned school.

Go north on Mason to San Diego Avenue, then turn east to Dodson's Corner.

Dodson's Corner is a group of false-front shops where merchants sometimes dress in period costume. Across San Diego Avenue is the San Diego Union Museum, home of the state's longest running newspaper.

From here go north on Twiggs Street to Calhoun Street.

At Calhoun you will see the Steelly Stables, and Blackhawk Smith and Stable, both worth a look.

Street art in the Gaslamp Quarter

Walk west on Calhoun to the Alvarado House and Johnson House, two beautiful and historic structures. Retrace your steps back to Mason Street, then head south to visit the Casa De Estudillo. After touring the Casa, step across the street back into Old Town Plaza to end your tour.

To complement your stroll through Old Town, you could visit the nearby Gaslamp Quarter, bound by Broadway, 4th, 6th and Harbor streets, which gives a comprehensive history of San Diego's architecture.

PRESIDIO PARK ✪✪

Formerly the fort here protected Mission San Diego de Alcala. The park is just up the hill from the centre of Old Town. As you sit on the benches scattered among the trees of this 50-acre park you will have wonderful views of the Old Town expanse. San Diego's landmark museum, the Junipero Serra, sits high atop the hill where California's first mission and presidio were founded. Spanish, Mexican and Native American aspects of San Diego's history are recalled with exhibits of furniture, clothing, household items and other artefacts of the past 200 years.

➕ 59B2
✉ 2727 Presidio Drive
☎ 619/297 3258
🕐 Park daily; Junipero Serra Museum Fri–Sun 10–4
👆 Cheap

Rhinos at San Diego Wild Animal Park, Escondido

SAN DIEGO WILD ANIMAL PARK ✪✪

The park, 30 miles northeast of San Diego, is known for its authentic re-creation of African and Asian terrain. Almost 2,500 endangered animals are presented here by the Zoological Society of San Diego. This 2,100-acre preserve features a five-mile monorail tour, Nairobi Village animal shows, hiking trails and botanical exhibits.

➕ 69E1
✉ Via Rancho Pkwy exit off I–15
☎ 619/234 6541
🕐 Daily 9–4
👆 Expensive (combination pass with San Diego Zoo)

SCRIPPS AQUARIUM AND INSTITUTE OF OCEANOGRAPHY ✪✪

Recently included as part of the University of California at San Diego, Scripps Aquarium and the Memorial Pier are landmarks of the La Jolla coast. Marine scientists have been working here since the turn of the century. The Institute displays the aquatic world in indoor tanks, an on-shore tidepool and through additional oceanographic exhibits showing the latest advances in oceanography.

➕ 59A3
✉ 8602 La Jolla Shores Drive
☎ 619/534 3474
🕐 Call ahead
👆 Free

🕂 59B2
✉ Sea World Drive off the
I–5, Mission Bay Park
☎ 619/226 3901
🕓 Mon–Fri 10–5, Sat, Sun
10–7
✋ Expensive

SEA WORLD ✪✪✪

Perhaps one of, if not *the* finest marine biology park in the world, Sea World is impressive, and you can and should plan on spending the better part of a day here. Comfortably spread out over 150 acres, it features continuous killer whale and dolphin shows, and highly informative marine life exhibits. Between shows, you can touch or view live animals in the petting pools. Also not to miss are the nautical theme playground, marina and state-of-the-art research laboratories.

Sea World is home to killer whales Shamu and Baby Shamu, the real stars of the park, as well as seals, sea lions and walruses. The Rocky Point Preserve is a habitat for dolphins and sea otters, while 'Penguin Encounter' has over 300 penguins. Other exhibits include 'Shark Encounter' and 'Forbidden Reef'. A family-oriented theme park features interactive games and adventures. Guided tours are available, and in the summer there are evening aquatic shows. Owing to the park's popularity, you can expect long waits for some shows and exhibits, especially during the summer.

Don't forget the re-entry stamp should you decide to leave the park and return later. Ticket sales stop 90 minutes before closing, which is around sunset most of the year, but up until 11PM in the summer.

*Sea World deserves a
whole day to do it justice*

A Drive From San Diego

This drive includes historic Route 1, the Palomar Observatory and the San Diego Wild Animal Park.

Leave downtown on Route 1, going north out of the city. Pass through La Jolla.

Stop to enjoy the view from the cliffs (➤ 60). Also recommended is a stop at Torrey Pines State Preserve, a 1,000-acre area which has one of the world's two surviving stands of the Torrey pine tree. The walking trails are unique and offer a pleasant break from driving.

Continue north through Del Mar (stop at the famous racetrack if you are here in the summer), and on to Solana Beach, and finally Carlsbad.

Carlsbad is one of many pleasant communities in Southern California and is a good place to stop for lunch and do some shopping.

Highway 1 now becomes the 5 Freeway, which you follow north to SR 78. Exit and proceed east on SR 78 through San Marcos and into Escondido.

Champagne Boulevard in Escondido (🕙 10–5) is the world's only combined winery and car museum, with over 100 American convertibles on display.

From Escondido take SR 17 east to the San Diego Wild Animal Park (➤ 63). Spend a few hours here before continuing on SR 17 to Ramona. At Ramona take the junction on to Highway 67, a beautiful route that takes you past the Barona Indian Reservation. It then becomes the 8 Freeway, returning to downtown San Diego.

Distance
60 miles

Time
About 5–7 hours, depending on time spent at attractions

Start/end point
Downtown San Diego
✚ 59A3

Lunch
Coyote Bar and Grill (£)
✉ 300 Carlsbad Village Drive
☎ 70/729 4695
🕙 Daily 11AM–2AM

A fine photo opportunity at San Diego Wildlife Park

Rest of California

With its diverse environments and cultures, and its progressive way of thinking, California is more like an independent country than a state. As unique and varied as the major cities are, the outlying regions are even more so. There are the sprawling green vineyards of Napa and Sonoma valleys, the giant trees of Yosemite, Redwood and Sequoia national parks, mountains, deserts, inland seas and, of course, the ocean. The communities themselves range from up-market urban centres like Palm Springs to unpretentious farming and manufacturing towns. The 21 mission communities are perhaps the most charming of all. Their distinctive architectural style features stone and adobe, with whitewashed mud plaster inside and out. The pitched roofs of hewn timber, covered with red tiles, bring elegance and historical import to the entire state.

' ... wonderful, wonderful, sublime, indescribable, incomprehensible; I never saw anything so truly and appallingly grand; it pays me a hundred times over for visiting California. '

P T BARNUM
after his first visit to California

———————•———————

View from the Sky Jump at Knotts Berry Farm, Anaheim

67

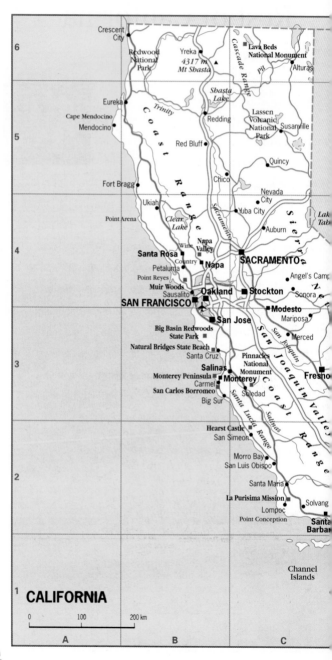

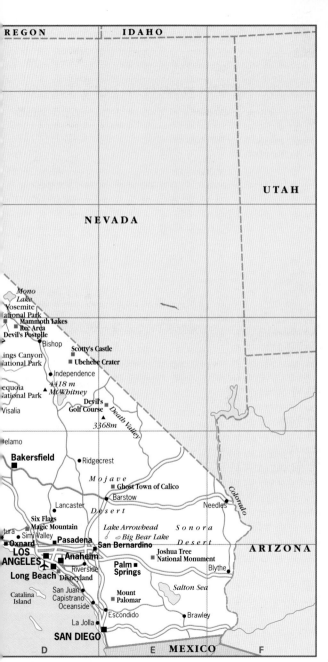

OREGON

IDAHO

UTAH

NEVADA

Mono Lake
Yosemite National Park
■ Mammoth Lakes
■ Rec Area
Devil's Postpile
● Bishop
Scotty's Castle
Kings Canyon National Park
■ Ubehebe Crater
● Independence
▲ *4418 m* Mt Whitney
Sequoia National Park
Devil's Golf Course
Death Valley
Visalia
▲ *3368m*

Delamo
Bakersfield
● Ridgecrest
Mojave
■ Ghost Town of Calico
● Lancaster
● Barstow
Desert
Needles
Colorado

Six Flags
Magic Mountain
Lake Arrowhead
Sonora
ventura ● Simi Valley
Pasadena
San Bernardino
Desert
Oxnard
◐ Big Bear Lake
LOS ANGELES
Anaheim
Joshua Tree
■ National Monument
ARIZONA
Long Beach
Riverside
Palm Springs
Disneyland
Blythe ●
Catalina Island
San Juan
Capistrano
Oceanside
Mount
■ Palomar
Salton Sea
La Jolla ●
● Escondido
● Brawley
SAN DIEGO
D
E
MEXICO
F

69

What to See in the Rest of California

ANAHEIM ✪✪
Anaheim was originally founded as the centre of a wine-producing colony by German immigrants in 1857. The vineyards were replaced by orange groves late in the 19th century, after an especially brutal drought. Oranges thrived until the 1950s, when commercial interests and the rapid growth of the Los Angeles metropolitan area took over. The two main attractions in the area are Disneyland (➤ 18) and Knott's Berry Farm (➤ 78).

🕂 69D1
✉ 46 miles from Los Angeles via I-5; directly across from Disneyland

BAKERSFIELD ✪
Bakersfield is California's main oil-producing centre. Many consider it a less-than-desirable part of California, its furnace-like, 100°F-plus summers a major drawback. However, the downtown area is a vital mix of restored buildings and newer offices. Of note in the town are a genuine schoolhouse, church and a fully restored 1868 log cabin.

The **California Living Museum** focuses on the state's wildlife and native plants, many of which have become rare or endangered.

Kern County Museum has exhibits representing both human and natural history of the area.

🕂 69D2
California Living Museum
✉ 14000 Alfred Harrell Highway
☎ 805/872 2256
🕐 Wed–Sun 9–4
🍴 Picnic facilities
👜 Cheap

Kern County Museum
✉ 3801 Chester Avenue
☎ 661/852 5000
🕐 Mon–Fri 8–5, Sat 10–5, Sun noon–5
👜 Cheap

BARSTOW ✪
Barstow is the halfway point between Los Angeles and Las Vegas. Settled in the early 19th century, silver mines flourished in the surrounding areas. The town of **Calico** boomed in the late 1800s, and its mines produced $15 million worth of ore. When the price of silver dropped, the town went bust. Today, you can visit the 'ghost town' of Calico to pan for gold, ride the steam railway or see a show at the Calikage Playhouse.

North of Barstow is **Rainbow Basin National Natural Landmark**, formed by the deposit of sediment over millions of years. Fossils, the forces of nature and an abundance of minerals give it its dramatic shapes and colours.

🕂 69E2
Calico Ghost Town
✉ 11 miles northeast of Barstow via I-15
☎ 760/254 2122
🕐 Daily 9–5
🍴 Restaurants moderate
👜 Moderate

Rainbow Basin National Natural Landmark
✉ Fossil Bed Road, 8 miles north of Barstow via SR 58

BIG BEAR LAKE ✪✪✪
One of California's largest and most popular recreation areas, the Big Bear Lake region has two distinct sections; Big Bear Lake, and Big Bear City, on the eastern end of the lake. Big Bear Village, centred around the lake, is popular for lodging, dining and shopping. Camping, hiking and horseback riding are available in summer, and skiing in winter.

🕂 69E2
✉ Big Bear Chamber of Commerce, 630 Bartlett Road, 92315
☎ 909/866 7000
🍴 Many restaurants (£–£££)

CARMEL ✪✪✪

Carmel was established in the late 19th century and has since gained its reputation as a bohemian retreat. It has

some of the most picturesque coastal residences in the state, many in Spanish-Mission style. **Mission San Carlos Borromeo del Rio Carmelo** (1769) was moved to its riverside site here in Carmel in 1771. Father Junípero Serra is buried in the church, which

was given the status of minor basilica by the Pope in 1960.

CATALINA ISLAND (➤ 16, TOP TEN)

DEATH VALLEY NATIONAL PARK ✪✪✪

Three million years ago, inner-earth forces tormented, twisted and shook the land in what is now Death Valley, creating snowcapped mountains and superheated valleys. Lakes, formed during the Ice Age, evaporated, leaving alternating layers of mud and salt deposits.

Over three million acres in size, Death Valley ranges in elevation from 282 feet below sea level to slightly over 11,000 above. Temperatures reach well over 100°F in summer, making it one of the hottest regions in the world.

Scotty's Castle, on the northern boundary of the park, is a Spanish/Moorish construction built by Chicago insurance tycoon Albert Johnson for Walter E Scott, alias 'Death Valley Scotty'.

✚ 68B3

Mission San Carlos Borromeo del Rio Carmelo
✉ 3080 Rio Road
☎ 408/624 1272
🕐 Mon–Sat 9:30–4:30, Sun 10:30–4:30
💵 Free, but donations accepted

Left: *Mission San Carlos Borromeo del Rio Carmelo, final resting place of Junípero Serra*
Below: *cycling at Big Bear Lake*

✚ 69E3
✉ Furnace Creek Visitors Center
☎ 760/786 3244
🕐 Daily 8–7
♿ Some areas handicap accessible
💵 Cheap
❓ Camping facilities

Scotty's Castle
☎ 760/786 2392
🕐 Daily 9–5
💵 Moderate

The beautiful Blossom Trail in the fruit orchards around Fresno

🞦 68B5
Clarke Memorial Museum
✉ Third and 'E' streets
☎ 707/443 1947
🕐 Tue–Sat noon–4
💰 Cheap

Blue Ox Millworks
✉ Foot of 'X' street
☎ 707/444 3437
🕐 Mon–Sat 9–5
💰 Cheap

Sequoia Park
✉ Glatt and 'W' Streets
☎ 707/442 6552
🕐 Daily 10am–dusk
🍴 Picnic facilities
💰 Cheap

🞦 68C3
Metropolitan Museum of Art, History and Science
✉ 1555 Van Ness Avenue
☎ 209/441 1444
🕐 Daily 11–5
💰 Cheap

🞦 68C4
Angel's Camp Museum
✉ 753 South Main Street
☎ 209/736 2963
🕐 Daily 10–3
💰 Cheap

EUREKA   ✪✪
Eureka is the largest town on California's northernmost coast. Set along Humboldt Bay, it is home to an impressive fishing fleet. Its name, from the Greek word for 'I have found it', refers to the cries from many gold miners (called '49ers) in the 19th century. The Old Town section is worth a visit for its elegantly refurbished Victorian homes.

The old 1912 building, once the town's main bank, now houses the **Clarke Memorial Museum**. It houses an excellent collection of California Native American historic artefacts.

Blue Ox Millworks is a working mill that includes a blacksmith shop and a re-creation of a logging camp. **Sequoia Park**, a beautiful grove of virgin redwoods in 52 acres, has a formal flower garden, duck pond, and deer and elk paddocks.

FRESNO   ✪✪
Fresno lies in the heart of the San Joaquin Valley. One of the foremost agricultural areas in the country, it is also the gateway to the Sierra Nevada's three national parks.

The town's fine **Metropolitan Museum of Art, History and Science** features an extensive collection of Asian art, as well as American still-life paintings. Wild Water Adventure Park, on E Shaw Avenue, contains over 20 water rides, pools and a small fishing lake.

GOLD COUNTRY TOWNS   ✪✪✪
Also known as the Mother Lode Country, this scenic area extends 300 miles along Highway 49, through the western Sierra Nevada foothills. Once the thriving Old West, it is now mostly ghost towns, several of which are open to tourists.

Angel's Camp Museum, in Angel's Camp (➤ 74), was the centre for gravel and quartz mining in 1849. You can see photographs, relics and three acres of old mining equipment from the old days.

Marshall Gold Discovery State Historic Park is where James Marshall discovered gold. The drive-through park features a replica of Sutter's Mill and memorial statue and grave site of James Marshall.

The Empire Mine State Historic Park (► 74), 2 miles east of Grass Valley, is the Gold Country's best preserved quartz mining operation. During the boom years, the 367 miles of mine shafts produced six million ounces of gold.

Mercer Caverns, 1 mile north of Murphys, via Main Street, were discovered in 1885 by Walter Mercer, a gold prospector. The 45-minute tour gives the opportunity to view the enormous stalagmites and stalactites close up.

Marshall Gold Discovery State Historic Park
- ⊠ North fork of the American River and Highway 49, Coloma
- ☎ 530/622 3470
- 🕐 Daily 8–sunset
- 💵 Cheap

JOSHUA TREE NATIONAL MONUMENT ⭐⭐⭐

Known for its distinctive Joshua trees (a desert tree of the yucca species), and its uniquely shaped rock formations, the park connects the 'high' and 'low' deserts.

Within the park is Key's View, a high elevation with incredible views on a clear day. Not to be missed is the Cholla Cactus Garden, about 10 miles south of the Oasis Visitors Center.

- ✚ 69E1
- ⊠ Oasis Vistors Center, National Monument Drive, 29 Palms
- ☎ 619/367 7511
- 🕐 Daily 8–4:30
- 💵 Cheap

Did you know ?

UFO devotees insist there is a secret starship base hidden somewhere in the brush-dotted hills of the park at Joshua Tree. At Giant Rock Airport (2477 Belfield, off Reches Road and Highway 247, Yucca Valley) you can visit a mysterious 40-foot dome, Integration, a showpiece for UFO cultists.

The striking Joshua tree is said to be so named because Western pioneers believed it resembled the biblical Joshua raising his arms to the heavens and stopping the sun so the Israelites could win their battle

A Drive Through the Gold Country

This drive will take you through Gold Country along historic Highway 49.

Begin in Mariposa, where SR 49 meets SR 140.

Here you can visit the California State Mining and Mineral Museum and the Mariposa County Museum.

Proceed north on SR 49 to Chinese Camp and the State Historic Park. A few miles north is Jamestown.

Gold was discovered in Jamestown in 1848

Jamestown served as a backdrop for the film *High Noon* and the television series *Little House on the Prairie*.

Follow 49 north, stopping in Tuttletown.

You can view a replica of Mark Twain's cabin on Jackass Hill (Tuttletown was originally called Jackass Gulch).

Continue to Columbia.

Here you can try your hand at panning for gold, or ride an authentic stagecoach.

Continue north on 49 to Angel's Camp.

This is where Mark Twain first heard the 'jumping frog' story from bartender Ben Coon. If you are here in May, don't miss the frog jumping contest. The foundation of Angel's Mine, one of the region's most profitable, can be found across from the Catholic Church.

Continue north to Jackson and Placerville.

Jackson was once home of the Mohawk Indians, and Placerville was formerly known as 'Hangtown'. Gold Bug Mine is worth a visit.

Further north are Coloma, Auburn and Grass Valley.

The latter is home to Empire Mine State Historic Park (► 73) and North Star Mine Museum, both offering tours.

The drive ends in Nevada City.

Distance
Approximately 100 miles

Time
8 hours

Start point
Mariposa
✚ 68C3

End point
Nevada City
✚ 68C4

Lunch
National Hotel Restaurant (£)
✉ 77 Main Street,
  Jamestown
☎ 209/984 3446

LAKE ARROWHEAD ✪✪

Known locally as a sophisticated mountain getaway, this is where LA's wealthy spend leisurely weekends in luxury homes. Restrictive development laws help preserve the area's natural beauty. Swimming and boating are popular activities in summer, and skiing in winter.

➕ 69E2
✉ Chamber of Commerce, Lake Arrowhead Village
☎ 909/337 3715
🕐 Mon–Fri 9–5
💰 Expensive

LAKE TAHOE ✪✪✪

Situated on the California–Nevada stateline, Lake Tahoe is one of the most popular resort communities in the state. Although this beautiful lake is 6,228 feet above sea level, it never freezes because of its depth. You will find top-notch ski areas here, and in summer, water sports include lake cruises, water skiing and sailing.

For a spectacular aerial view of the entire area, including the site of the 1960 Winter Olympic Games, ride the gondola to the top of the Squaw Valley Ski Area.

➕ 68C4
Squaw Valley Cable Car
✉ 1960 Squaw Valley Road, Olympic Valley
☎ 530/583 6985
🕐 Call to check. Closed mid Oct–1 Dec
💰 Moderate

Bumpass Hell, at Lassen

LASSEN VOLCANIC NATIONAL PARK ✪✪✪

Lassen Park stretches over 100,000 acres in the north-eastern corner of California, where the Cascade and Sierra Nevada mountains meet. Points of interest are Lassen Peak, Cinder Cone, Prospect Peak and Mount Harkness, the latter two volcanoes topped by cinder cones.

Lassen's numerous volcanic eruptions subsided in 1921 and have been replaced by inviting hot springs and lakes, lava flows and mudpots, all linked together by hiking trails that lead to the summit and back.

➕ 68C5
✉ 9 miles east of Mineral, via SR 36
☎ 530/595 4444
🕐 Year-round
💰 Cheap

MAMMOTH LAKES RECREATION AREA ✪✪

This giant popular resort area in the Inyo National Forest has world-class skiing, and in summertime it's a mountain biking mecca. There is also good camping, fishing and horseback riding here. Hike to the 101-foot Rainbow Falls, or visit the Devil's Postpile National Monument, 60-foot multi-sided columns that are by-products of former volcanic activity.

➕ 69D3
✉ Chamber of Commerce, PO Box 123, Mammoth Lakes, 93546
☎ 760/934 3068
🕐 Weekdays 9–5
🍴 Restaurants (££)
💰 Moderate

75

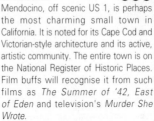

Mendocino Chamber of Commerce
+ 68A5
✉ 735 Main Street
☎ 800/276 2780
🕐 Daily 11–4
💲 Cheap

Mendocino Art Center
✉ 45200 Little Lake Street
☎ 707/937 5818 or 800/653 3328
🕐 Call for times
💲 Moderate

+ 68C4
McHenry Museum & Mansion
✉ 1402 'I' Street
☎ 209/577 5366 (museum); 577 5341 (mansion)
🕐 Tue–Sun noon–4. Closed major holidays
💲 Free, donations requested
❓ Tours of the mansion offered Tue–Thu and Sun 1–4, Fri noon–3

+ 68C2
✉ Chamber of Commerce, 80 Main Street #A–1, 93442
☎ 805/772 4467
🕐 Weekdays 9–5
💲 Free

Museum of Natural History
✉ Morro Bay State Park
☎ 805/772 2694
🕐 Daily 10–5
💲 Cheap

Tiger's Folly Cruises
✉ 1205 Embarcadero
☎ 805/772 2257
🕐 Call for schedules
💲 Cheap

MENDOCINO

Mendocino, off scenic US 1, is perhaps the most charming small town in California. It is noted for its Cape Cod and Victorian-style architecture and its active, artistic community. The entire town is on the National Register of Historic Places. Film buffs will recognise it from such films as *The Summer of '42*, *East of Eden* and television's *Murder She Wrote*.

The **Art Center** is the epicentre of the many art museums in the community, and includes galleries, live theatre and arts and craft fairs.

MODESTO

This quintessential California town was made famous by George Lucas's film *American Graffiti*. Near the centre of the state, it is the home of the Blue Diamond Almonds company.

The **McHenry Museum** re-creates a 19th-century school, blacksmith shop, kitchen, country store and others with changing exhibits. The **McHenry Mansion**, a block away, exhibits antique furnishings and artwork in a restored Victorian home.

MONTEREY PENINSULA (▶ 22, TOP TEN)

MORRO BAY

Morro Rock, the conical, volcano-shaped rock that towers 578 feet out of the Pacific Ocean, sits guarding the entrance to Morro Bay, which is known primarily for its commercial fishing and oyster farming. Although the town has a modest tourist trade, the locals are mostly concerned with the daily business of fishing. Beneath the rock stretches a 5-mile-long beach with 85-foot-high white sand dunes that serve as a habitat for bird and plant life

The Morro Bay Arts Festival takes place each weekend in October, and the **Museum of Natural History** exhibits marine life native to the central coast, including the Bay's entertaining sea lions. **Tiger's Folly Cruises** offers harbour cruises.

The State Park, south of Morro Bay, is beautiful and a must for those who enjoy camping and hiking. The campgrounds are at the southern end of the park surrounded by cypress and eucalyptus.

The Galley Restaurant serves delicious seafood meals.

MOUNT PALOMAR ✪✪✪

Palomar Observatory houses the world-famous 200-inch Hale telescope. High above the distracting, bright city lights, the observatory also has several smaller telescopes, used to monitor the planet's movement. The small Greenway Museum contains photographs of the observatory's celestial sightings.

MOUNT SHASTA ✪✪

Spiritual-minded Californians flock to this mountain because it is said to be a 'vortex of spiritual energy'. For the more earthbound there is hiking, climbing, and skiing in winter. Several surrounding lakes offer waterside camping, fishing and watersports, including skating in winter.

The **Mount Shasta State Fish Hatchery**, in the centre of the area, produces 5 to 10 million trout annually to stock Northern California lakes.

OAKLAND ✪✪

Linked to San Francisco by the Bay Bridge, Oakland has long suffered from its close proximity to the city across the bay. In reality, it is a culturally rich and diversified town and has counted among its famous citizens Jack London and Gertrude Stein. **Oakland Museum** has an extensive collection of historical and contemporary art housed in the Gallery of California Art. The museum is one of the best in the state for studying the diverse cultural make-up and subsequent historical progress.

Lake Merritt, created in the late 19th century by the damming of a section of the Oakland estuary, was one of the first natural wildlife preserves established in the country.

➕ 69E1
✉ 4½ miles north of San Diego on SR 6
☎ 619/742 2119
🕐 Daily 9–4
🎟 Free

➕ 68B6
✉ Chamber of Commerce Visitors Bureau, 300 Pine Street, 96067
☎ 530/926 6212 or 800/926 4865

Mount Shasta State Fish Hatchery
☎ 916/926 2215
🕐 Daily 7am–dusk
🎟 Free

➕ 68B4

Oakland Museum
✉ 11th and Oak Street
☎ 510/238 2200
🕐 Wed–Sat 10–5, Sun noon–7
🎟 Cheap

Mount Shasta is usually snow-capped all year

77

Orange County

Known by Californians as the 'conservative' enclave of the state, Orange County is a sprawling, seemingly endless expanse of humanity between Los Angeles and San Diego, with its own unique charms.

DISNEYLAND (➤ 18, TOP TEN)

FESTIVAL OF THE ARTS/PAGEANT OF THE MASTERS   ✪✪

A 'state-of-the-art' art exhibit in the scenic wooded Laguna Canyon, this is a landmark event, the former featuring an exhibit of 150 Laguna artists of all kinds. The most interesting aspect of this seven-week event, however, is the Pageant of the Masters, in which human models stand perfectly still for three minutes in re-creations of famous paintings and sculptures, with a musical accompaniment.

HUNTINGTON ART CENTER   ✪

Though small, the Huntington Art Center is concerned with local contemporary art and architecture in a big way. It has been recently renovated and is a favourite with many local artists. Films are shown the first and third Friday of each month.

INTERNATIONAL SURFING MUSEUM   ✪✪

Huntington Beach calls itself 'Surf City', with good reason, and is a mecca for surfing enthusiasts. Exhibits tell the sport's history, and the store sells surf gear, all, of course, to the music of the Beach Boys.

KNOTT'S BERRY FARM   ✪✪✪

One of California's original theme parks, Knott's has grown from a true berry farm to a modern 150-acre attraction with over 165 rides. The Western theme areas include Ghost Town and Gold Mine Ride. Other attractions include Camp Snoopy, Wild Water Wilderness, Mystery Lodge, Reflection Lake, California Marketplace and Kingdom of the Dinosaurs. For the adventurous, there are four 'awesome' rollercoasters, the Boomerang, Montezooma's Revenge, the Jaguar and the Windjammer. And, finally, for the truly hungry, Knott's serves its original, delicious, world-famous boysenberry pie.

LAGUNA ART MUSEUM   ✪✪✪

The Laguna Art Museum was founded in 1918 and is the showcase venue for the Laguna Art Association. It usually features several visiting exhibits of paintings and sculpture by California artists. On permanent display are historical California landscapes and vintage photographs of the region.

Sidebar info:

🔲 Off map 47E1
✉ Laguna Canyon Road, Laguna Beach
☎ 714/494 1145
🕐 Jul–Aug 10AM–11PM
💲 Expensive

🔲 47D1
✉ Main Street E, Huntington Beach
☎ 714/374 1650
🕐 Daily noon–6, Thu–Fri until 9:30, Sun until 4
💲 Free

🔲 47D1
✉ Olive Street, ½ block off Main, Huntington Beach
☎ 714/960 3483
🕐 Daily 10–6
💲 Cheap

🔲 47E2
✉ 8039 Beach Boulevard, Buena Park
☎ 714/220 5200
🕐 Subject to change; call for current times
💲 Expensive

🔲 Off map 47E1
✉ Pacific Coast Highway and Cliff Drive, Laguna Beach
☎ 714/759 1122
🕐 Tue–Sun 11–5
💲 Cheap

MISSION SAN JUAN CAPISTRANO ✪✪✪

Founded in 1776, this is one of California's most beautiful missions, and the only building still standing where Father Serra said mass. On 19 March each year, the Feast of St Joseph celebrates the legendary 'return of the swallows'.

➕ 69D1
✉ 26701 Verdugo Street
☎ 714/248 2048
🕐 Daily 8:30–5
✋ Cheap

Did you know ?

The swallows of San Juan Capistrano have the reputation of returning every 19 March. In reality, they return over a period of several weeks. They leave their winter home in South America around 23 October on their 6,000-mile flight 'home' to spend spring and summer in Southern California.

Mission San Juan Capistrano, the seventh of the California missions

SHERMAN LIBRARY AND GARDENS ✪✪

The unique gardens here are filled with orchids and koi ponds, while the library itself is a large building, taking up a whole city block. It functions as a centre of historical research for the region. There is an extensive collection of historical Orange County documents and photographs.

➕ Off map 47E1
✉ 2647 E Coast Highway, Newport Beach
☎ 714/673 2261
🕐 Mon–Fri 9–4:30
✋ Cheap. Free Mon

YORBA LINDA ✪✪

The Richard Nixon Presidential Library and Birthplace, in Yorba Linda, has galleries, theatres and gardens, and personal memorabilia of this former US president. The grounds feature the small house where he was born, his post-presidency private study and a re-creation of the White House's Lincoln Sitting Room.

➕ 47F2
✉ 18001 Yorba Linda Boulevard
☎ 714/993 5075
🕐 Mon–Sat 10–5, Sun 11–5.
✋ Moderate

In the Know

Ways To Be A Local

Dress casual but trendy. Sunwear and leather in the south; tie-dyed wear in San Francisco; hiking boots and jeans in the north.

Carry a cellular phone and/or pager.

In Los Angeles, talk about movie deals.

In San Francisco, talk about the fog.

In San Diego and the desert areas, don't talk, just smile in a laid-back manner.

Absolutely no one walks in Los Angeles, so rent a convertible, or better still, a Mercedes convertible.

Eat light and healthy meals like salads, pasta and fresh fruit, accompanied by a glass of Californian wine.

Safeguard yourself and your valuables. In major cities, lock your car doors while driving. At the beaches, don't carry your wallet in your back pocket.

California-speak is as casual as the lifestyle, and often includes a Mexican word or two. Say Ro-DAY-oh (Rodeo), Si-PUL-vi-dah (Sepulveda), and La Con-YAH-dah (La Cañada). But don't worry if you slip into your native tongue, you hear almost every language in the world here.

Carry a bottle of water with you at all times; 'foreign' water is the 'coolest'.

Ceviche – a popular seafood dish

Good Places To Have Lunch

Gladstones 4 Fish (£) Fresh seafood on the beach.
✉ 17300 Pacific Coast Highway, Pacific Palisade, Los Angeles ☎ 310/GL4 FISH, 310/454 3474

MargaritaVille (££) Local favourite for authentic Mexican food, but also serves American food. ✉ 2332 W Coast Highway, San Diego ☎ 714/631 8220

Pinks Hot Dog Stand (£) Grunge stand with limo parking and great dogs and burgers.
✉ Highland and Melrose, Los Angeles

Louise's Trattatoria (£££) Very trendy, with some of the best pasta in the city.
✉ 7505 Melrose Avenue, Los Angeles
☎ 213/651 3880

Karl Strauss' Old Columbia Brewery & Grill (££) Specialities are burgers, fresh fish and German-style sausage. Watch the microbrewery process while you sip a cold one.

✉ 1157 Columbia Street, San Diego ☎ 619/234 2739

The Bakery (£) (➤ 99)
✉ 129 E Anapumu, Santa Barbara ☎ 805/962 2089

Cadillac Bar & Restaurant (££)
✉ One Holland Court, San Francisco ☎ 415/543 8226

Pier 23 Café (££)
✉ The Embarcadero (Pier 23) at Broadway, San Francisco ☎ 415/362 5125

Carmel Café (£)
Quaint, clean and breakfast served all day long.
✉ Mission between 5th & 6th, Carmel ☎ 408/624 1922

Fat City Café and Bar (£–££)
Art nouveau, old European atmosphere with stained glass and a 100-year-old bar. Light entrées and rich desserts.
✉ 1001 Front Street, Sacramento ☎ 916/446 6769

10
Top Activities

• **Surfing**
• **Exercising** at a gym or health club, or by doing yoga, karate or ta'i chi
• **Hiking/backpacking**
• **Going to the movies**
• **Cycling**
• **Rollerblading**
• **Boating** (all kinds)
• **Golfing**
• **Going to the** theme parks
• **Attending concerts** from rock to jazz to classical

10
Unique Annual Events

• National Date Festival and Fair (camel and ostrich races), Indio, February (☎ 619/863 8247)
• Snowfest (West's largest), Tahoe City, March (☎ 916/583 7625)
• Mendocino/Fort Bragg Whale Festival, March (☎ 707/961 6300)
• Frog Jumping Contest, Angel's Camp, May (☎ 209/736 2561)
• Dixieland Jazz Jubilee, Sacramento, May (☎ 916/372 5277)
• Great Monterey Squid Festival, Monterey, May (☎ 408/649 6544)
• Gilroy Garlic Festival, Gilroy, July (☎ 408/842 1625)
• Grand National Rodeo, Horse, and Stock Show, Daly City (world-class), October (☎ 415/469 6057)
• Doo Dah Parade (spoof of famous Rose Parade), Pasadena, November (☎ 626/449 3689)
• Monarch butterfly migration to Pismo Beach's Butterfly Trees, November to March

10
California Specialties

• Sit-ins
• Sun and surf
• San Francisco hippies
• Spiritual seekers
• Sonoma and Napa Valley wines
• Stars (human, not celestial)
• Smog
• Smoking prohibitions
• San Andreas fault
• Sequoias

Rafting on the Stanislaus River

➕ 69D2

Carnegie Art Museum

✉ 424 S 'C' Street

☎ 805/385 8157

🕐 Thu and Sat 10–5, Fri 11–6, Sun 1–5

💷 Cheap

Ventura County Gull Wings Children's Museum

✉ 418 W 4th Street

☎ 805/483 3005

🕐 Wed–Fri 1–5, Sat 10–5

💷 Cheap

➕ 69E1

Anza-Borrego Desert State Park

✉ Visitors Center, 2 miles west of Borrego Springs Township

☎ 760/767 5311

🕐 Call for hours and more information

💷 Cheap

Agua Caliente Indian Reservation

☎ 760/325 5673

🕐 Daily 8–6

💷 Cheap

Palm Springs Aerial Tramway

✉ Tramway Road, 3 miles southwest of SR 111

☎ 760/325 1391

🕐 Mon–Fri 10–9, Sat–Sun 8–9. Closed 2 weeks in Aug

💷 Moderate

Resident of the Agua Caliente Indian Reservation

OXNARD ✪

Oxnard is a harbour town located on the Ventura–Los Angeles county line, and is home to an annual Strawberry Festival each May. Surpisingly overlooked by visitors are the 7 miles of beautiful beaches lining the town.

The **Carnegie Art Museum** has a permanent collection of 20th-century California painters, while changing exhibits feature photography and sculpture, with some shows spotlighting local artists.

The **Ventura County Gull Wings Children's Museum**'s hands-on exhibits of fossils and minerals, including a puppet theatre and make-believe campground, will entertain the kids.

PALM SPRINGS ✪✪✪

Rising out of the desert like on oasis, Palm Springs is one of the most famous resort towns in the world. It has become a favourite of wealthy retirees with a penchant for good golf and bad driving habits, and an ever-increasing number of young people are looking here for a brief spring retreat from their studies. The summers are insufferably hot, however, and the population dwindles from June through early September.

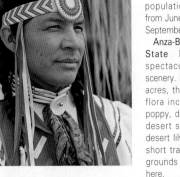

Anza-Borrego Desert State Park offers spectacular desert scenery. Set in 600,000 acres, the park's main flora includes lupine, poppy, dune primrose, desert sunflower and desert lily. A variety of short trails and campgrounds can be found here.

Five miles south of Palm Springs is **Agua Caliente Indian Reservation**. The Tribal Council here has opened a large portion of the reservation for hiking and picnics.

An awesome view of the San Jacinto Mountains awaits if you ride the **Palm Springs Aerial Tramway**, almost 5,000 feet straight up. The perfect way to escape the debilitating summer heat, you ride up to the wooded trails and campgrounds at the top, where refreshments are available.

PETALUMA ✪✪

Petaluma is another one of the quintessential small California towns. Situated on the Petaluma River, it has retained most of its 19th-century architecture and, like Modesto (➤ 76), has become a favourite for filming television series and movies.

Philanthropist Andrew Carnegie endowed $12,500 toward the construction of the **Historical Museum/Library** in 1903. It houses permanent and rotating exhibits of early 19th-century Petaluma.

REDWOOD NATIONAL PARK (➤ 25, TOP TEN)

RIVERSIDE ✪

Because the region has the ideal climate and soil for growing navel oranges, this was the wealthiest US city per capita and the metropolitan centre of Southern California at the turn of the century. Several buildings remain from around this time: the Italian Renaissance-style City Hall, the Classic Revival municipal museum, and many exquisite Victorian homes. In addition, mission architecture and adobe residences still reflect the early wealth and prestige.

California Citrus State Historic Park features a grove of 80 varieties of citrus trees. The visitor centre is a Victorian house typical of the city's heyday era. The Riverside Municipal Museum, at 3720 Orange Street, traces the history of citrus-growing in the region.

✚ 68B4

Petaluma Historical Museum/Library
✉ 20 4th Street
☎ 707/778 4398
🕐 Thu–Mon noon–4
💲 Cheap

✚ 69D1

California Citrus State Historic Park
✉ Van Buren Boulevard at Dufferin Avenue
☎ 909/780 6222
🕐 Daily 8–3
🍴 Picnic facilities
💲 Free

Palm Springs Aerial Tramway

The carefully restored State Capitol Building, centre of California's government

SACRAMENTO ✪✪

Sacramento was once a major supply centre for the California '49ers (gold seekers); now it is the state capital. The names of 5,822 Californians killed in the Vietnam War are engraved on the 22 black granite panels of the California Vietnam Veterans Memorial, near the State Capitol Park.

The exquisite **Governor's Mansion** dates from the 1800s and is now a museum of Victoriana. Items from former governors include a 1902 Steinway piano and Persian carpets.

The Historic Paddlewheeler *Spirit of Sacramento* is available for a Sacramento River cruise or special events. The boat's murder-mystery trips on the *Spirit* are especially popular.

A million-dollar gold collection, ethnic photos and a historic print shop are just some of the items in the five separate areas of the **Discovery Museum**. The **California State Railroad Museum** has three entire floors devoted to railroad-related exhibits, including train cars and 21 locomotives.

Noted for its 210-foot dome, the **State Capitol** building is nearly 150 years old, and is open daily for tours. Adobe-style **Sutter's Fort** was the first European outpost in California and contains some very interesting period relics.

Sacramento Zoo has a large reptile display and 350 species of wild animals.

The Towe Ford Museum and Waterworld USA (➤ 111) are also worth visiting.

✚ 68C4
Governor's Mansion State Historic Park
✉ 16th & 'H' streets
☎ 916/323 3047
🕐 Daily 10–4
👋 Cheap

Spirit of Sacramento
✉ Old Sacramento's 'L' Street Landing
☎ 916/552 2933
🕐 Cruises Wed–Sun 1:30 and 3 in summer, Fri–Sun spring and autumn
🍴 Dinner, brunch and happy hour cruises available
👋 Moderate

Discovery Museum
✉ 101 'I' Street
☎ 916/264 7057
🕐 Tue–Sun 10–5 summers; Tue–Fri noon–5, Sat–Sun 10–5
👋 Cheap

California State Railroad Museum
✉ Second & 'I' streets
☎ 916/445 4209; 448 4466 for recorded information
🕐 Daily 10–5
👋 Moderate

State Capitol
✉ Between 10th, 15h, 'L' and 'N' streets
☎ 916/324 0333
🕐 Daily 9–5
👋 Free

Sutter's Fort
✉ 27th & 'L' streets
☎ 916/445 4422
🕐 Daily 10–5
👋 Moderate summers, cheap winters

Sacramento Zoo
✉ Sutterville Road
☎ 916/2264 5885
🕐 Daily 10–4
👋 Cheap

SALINAS ✪

John Steinbeck was born in this working-class town, 17 miles inland from Monterey. While it's sometimes overlooked in favour of its more affluent neighbours, Salinas is charming. For those visiting in August, there is the Steinbeck Festival. Many rodeo fans visit the town in July to catch one of the major stops on the professional rodeo circuit.

The *Hat In Three Stages of Landing* is a unique giant sculpture by Claes Oldenberg which captures a trio of bright yellow hats, each weighing 3,500 pounds. The sculpture graces the lawn of the Community Center where there are art exhibits and musical/theatrical performances.

SAN JOSE ✪✪

Surprisingly, San Jose is the 11th largest city in the US. It was founded in the last quarter of the 18th century as El Pueblo de San Jose, and is the oldest Spanish civilian settlement. From 1849 to 1851 it served as the state's capital.

Kelley Park, apart from being a popular city park with such attractions as Happy Hollow family play area and zoo, also contains the Japanese Friendship Garden and Teahouse and the San Jose Historical Museum.

Babylonian, Sumerian and Assyrian artefacts, mummies, sculptures and more can be found at the **Rosicrucian Egyptian Museum and Planetarium**. There is also a contemporary art gallery.

The **Winchester Mystery House**, a Victorian mansion and home of eccentric firearms heiress, Sarah Winchester, was designed to confuse evil spirits. The layout of the house is so complex, with blind closets, secret passageways, 13 bathrooms and 40 staircases, that even Sarah herself needed a map to find her way around.

Overlooking the Santa Clara Valley from the 4,209-foot summit of Mount Hamilton is the **Lick Observatory**.

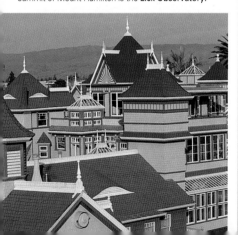

The bizarre Winchester House – a maze but well worth the tour price

---

🗺 68B3

Hat In Three Stages of Landing
✉ 940 N Main
☎ 408/758 7351
🕐 Mon–Fri 8–5
💲 Free

🗺 68B3

Kelley Park
✉ Senter and Story roads
☎ 408/277 5738
🕐 Daily 8 to 30 minutes before dusk
🍴 Picnic facilities
💲 Cheap

Rosicrucian Egyptian Museum and Planetarium
✉ Park Avenue between Naglee and Randol
☎ 408/947 3636
🕐 Daily 9–5
💲 Moderate; senior/student rates

Winchester Mystery House
✉ 525 S Winchester Boulevard
☎ 408/247 2101
🕐 Summer, daily 9–5:30; Labor Day through Oct, Mon–Fri 9–4, Sat–Sun 9–4:30; rest of year, daily 9:30–4 . Closed Christmas
💲 Expensive

Lick Observatory
✉ Mount Hamilton Road
☎ 408/274 5061
🕐 Daily 12:30–5
🍴 No nearby food or auto services
💲 Free

SANTA ANA ⊙⊙

A typical thriving small city in Orange County, Santa Ana centres around the South Coast Plaza, a European-styled mall with shops, restaurants and cinemas. The **Bowers Museum of Cultural Art**, a mission-style museum, is the largest in Orange County. It focuses on American, Pacific and African art, with an impressive permanent collection and quarterly visiting exhibits.

✚ 69E1

Bowers Museum of Cultural Art
✉ 2002 N Main Street
☎ 714/567 3600
🕐 Tue–Sun 10–4, Thu until 9
💷 Cheap

Mission Santa Barbara, often called the Queen of the Missions

SANTA BARBARA ⊙⊙⊙

A pleasant and affordable day trip from Los Angeles by train (moderate cost) taking you along the Pacific coast in the morning, gives you time to explore the historic adobes and museums. Lunch on Stearns Wharf, explore the speciality shops there, then stroll the white-sand beach, or play a short round of golf before returning in late afternoon. The County Courthouse, on Anacapa Street, is one of the best examples of Spanish-Moorish architecture in the US.

El Presidio de Santa Barbara State Historic Park, on the site of a late-1700 Spanish outpost, includes historical buildings such as El Cuartel, the second-oldest surviving edifice in California.

Mission Santa Barbara is the best preserved of the 21 California missions, and the church is filled with Mexican art from the 18th and 19th centuries. A Moorish fountain from 1808 graces the front and the mission is the site of The Little Fiesta each August.

The **Santa Barbara Museum of Art** has a wide variety of American, Asian and 19th-century French, Greek and Roman antiquities, including a major photographic collection.

Visit the Zoological Gardens which are natural habitats for 600 animals, and feature over 80 exhibits.

✚ 68C2
El Presidio de Santa Barbara State Historic Park
✉ 122–129 E Canon Perdido Street
☎ 805/966 9719
🕐 Daily 10:30–4:30; closed major holidays
💷 Free

Mission Santa Barbara
✉ E Los Olivos and Laguna Street
☎ 805/682 4149
🕐 Daily 9–5; closed major holidays
💷 Cheap, under 16 free

Museum of Art
✉ 1130 State Street
☎ 805/963 4364
🕐 Tue–Sat 11–5, Thu to 9; Sun noon–5; closed major holidays
💷 Cheap. Free Thu and 1st Sun of month

SIMI VALLEY ★★

The main reason for visiting Simi Valley is to see the **Ronald Reagan Presidential Library**, set in a beautiful, Spanish mission-style, hilltop mansion. Among the exhibits are photographs and memorabilia of the former US president's life, a full-scale replica of the Oval Office and a large portion of the Berlin Wall.

SOLEDAD ★

Soledad, the oldest settlement in the Salinas Valley, was established in 1791 with the founding of **Mission Nuestra Señora de la Soledad**, 3 miles west on US 101. The ruins of this adobe mission, along with a restored chapel and museum, can be seen to the east of town.

SOLVANG ★★★

Denmark in California might best describe Solvang, with its Danish architecture, windmills, gaslights and cobblestone walks. A tour of Solvang is possible in a horse-drawn Danish streetcar, and the town hosts several remarkable festivals annually. Contrasting the Scandinavian motif is the **Old Mission Santa Ines**, founded in 1804.

Typical Solvang architecture

VENTURA ★

This small beach town between Los Angeles and Santa Barbara is worth a brief visit.

San Buenaventura Mission was founded in 1782. The church is restored and the museum exhibits Native American artefacts from the Chumash tribes.

Albinger Archaeological Museum displays over 3,500 years of remains, all from areas around the Mission, while Ventura County Museum of History and Art has Native American, Hispanic and pioneer exhibits.

✚ 69D2
Ronald Reagan Presidential Library
✉ 40 Presidential Drive
☎ 805/522 8444
🕐 Daily 10–5; closed major holidays
✋ Cheap

✚ 68C3
Mission Nuestra Senora de la Soledad
✉ Fort Romie Road
☎ 408/678 2586
🕐 Wed–Mon 10–4
✋ Donations

✚ 68C2
✉ Chamber of Commerce, 1511 Mission Drive
☎ 805/688 0701 or 800/468 6765
🍴 Scandinavian restaurants and cafés (£–£££)

Old Mission Santa Ines
✉ 1760 Mission Drive
☎ 805/688 4815
🕐 May–Oct, daily 9–5; rest of year, 9–4:30; closed major holidays
✋ Cheap

✚ 69D2

San Buenaventura Mission
✉ 225 E Main Street
☎ 805/648 4496
🕐 Mon–Sat 10–5, Sun 10–4; closed major holidays
✋ Cheap

+ 68B4

Napa Valley Visitors Bureau

✉ 1310 Napa Town Centre, Napa 94559

☎ 707/226 7459

🕐 Hours vary; some tours require reservations

Sonoma Valley Visitors Bureau

✉ 453 1st Street, E Sonoma

☎ 707/996 1090

🕐 Daily 9–5

Napa Valley Wine Train

☎ 707/253 2111 or 800/427 4124

🕐 Year-round

💺 Expensive, reservations and deposit required

THE WINE COUNTRY

North of San Francisco lie some of the most lush valleys in all of California, the best known of which are the Napa (► 24) and Sonoma Valleys. It is here that California's vintners tend their grape vines and produce the many varied wines known and enjoyed world-wide. Whether you are driving, bicycling, taking the Wine Train or flying over the area in one of the many hot air balloons that offer spectacular views of the verdant, rolling, wine lands, you will never forget your excursion to the Wine Country.

The estates of the wineries are incredible to see. Take one of the guided tours of the processing facilities with their informative, enticing tastings. While the large wineries are the most popular, don't pass up the small, family-owned ones, of which there are many. Most have wines that rival the greats, with more convivial atmospheres.

The Napa Valley Wine Train provides daily excursions through the Napa Valley. The 1917 Pullman Dining Car relives the gracious era of elegant rail travel and distinguished service and makes you feel as if you're riding the Orient Express as the three-hour, 36-mile trip between Napa and St Helena allows for a leisurely brunch, lunch or dinner. Many concerns are aired by residents that the wineries are a bit too commercial for the area, but there are rarely complaints from the visitors.

To the west, the Sonoma Valley runs for 15 miles and is a bit less populated than the Napa Valley. As a rule, the 30 or so wineries here offer more personalised tours, with free tastings and a more relaxed atmosphere. The town of Sonoma itself is a good place to start if you wish to visit the valley. The other centre of activity is Santa Rosa, to the

*Above and opposite:
reaping the rewards of
a perfect climate.
Harvesting grapes in
Alexander Valley, Sonoma*

north of the region.

The Sonoma Valley is particularly rich in Spanish and Mexican history, so be sure to take note of the area's beautiful architecture.

If you're looking for souvenirs of your visit to California, the on-site gift shops have unique offerings and superb wines they will ship anywhere in the world. The wineries listed are just some of the ones you'll want to explore. *Spotlight's Wine Guide* is a complete guide to the area (☎ 415/898 7908).

CALIFORNIA DREAMIN'
You can explore the backroads of Northern California, including the Wine Country, in a range of classic convertibles on a guided trip with 'California Dreamin' Topless Tours'. Cars include a '97 Dodge Viper, BMW Z-3, Porsche Spyder and Shelby Cobra. Five-day tours begin and end in San Francisco.

☎ 707/426 0705

BERINGER VINEYARDS
Beringer was one of the very first wineries to open its cellar doors to visitors. The staff here are especially attentive and knowledgeable in discussing the process of wine making and its history.

✉ Just north of downtown St Helena
☎ 707/963 8989
🕐 Daily 9:30–4:30

BUENA VISTA WINERY
As the site of the first vineyard in the valley, Buena Vista, 2 miles northeast of Sonoma, has become a historical landmark. The wine cellars are the oldest stone cellars in the state.

✉ Old Winery Road
☎ 707/938 1266
🕐 Jul–Sep, daily 10:30–5; rest of year, 10:30–4:30

GLEN ELLEN WINERY
This century-old winery has recently opened a tasting room and history centre. Visitors are encouraged to enjoy the photographs, artefacts and other historical pieces that trace back a hundred years of wine making.

✉ Jack London Village, 14301 Arnold Drive, Glen Ellen
☎ 707/939 6277
🕐 Daily 10–5
🍴 Picnicking permitted
👆 Free

Did you know ?
Over a century ago, Hungarian Agoston Haraszthy planted the first vineyard in California, near the small town of Sonoma, seeding it with the best European grapes he could find. The state gave him funding, but neither envisioned the huge industry that would spring from his venture.

A Walk in Sequoia National Park

Distance
5 miles

Time
2–4 hours

Start point
General Sherman Tree
✚ 69D3

End point
General Sherman or Long Meadow
✚ 69D3

Lunch
Grant Grove Restaurant (££)
✉ Grant Grove Visitors Centre
☎ 2 09/335 2856

Whole groves of giants flourish in Sequoia

This walk takes you through the forest of Sequoia National Park. Even if you visit during the heat of the summer, you will find the temperatures comfortably cool because of the towering foliage.

Begin at the General Sherman Tree, 2 miles east of Giant Forest Village.

The General Sherman tree (named for the Civil War general) is 275 feet high. It is estimated to be more than 2,500 years old and contains enough wood to build 40 houses.

Walk down the self-guided, paved Congress Trail. Cross Sherman Creek on the quaint wooden bridge.

Experience the awesome giant sequoias, like the character-laden Leaning Tree and some lightning-struck and fire-scarred trees as well.

About a mile further along, you will meet the junction with the Alta Trail and reach a grove known as The Senate. A short distance further along the fern-filled trail is The House Grove.

These two stands are named after the two governing bodies of the United States government. The path also visits the McKinley Tree (named for the US president). After World War II, the park service abandoned the practice of naming big trees after politicos.

Continue a half-mile back, and return to the trail head. For a longer hike (about six miles), follow the Congress Trail to the junction of The Trail of the Sequoias. Take this path for a half-mile to the hike's high point, then gradually descend one and a half miles into Long Meadow.

Lunch before, or after, your hike at Giant Forest Village.

Where To...

Above: *City Lights bookstore, North Beach*
Right: *Fisherman's Wharf is the place to go for fresh seafood in San Francisco*

San Francisco

Prices
Average meal per head
excluding drink:
£ = up to $15
££ = between $15 and
$25
£££ = over $25

Good Old Dishes
The local cuisine of San
Francisco dates back to
the Gold Rush days. Old
faithful dishes such as
cioppino (seafood
casserole), hangtown fry
(oysters dipped in egg and
flour and fried with bacon),
fortune cookies and Irish
coffee are among the
most famous. Most fresh
fish is grilled with a bit of
Slavic, or French,
influence.

Alfred's (££)
Quintessential steakhouse
with bordello-like setting.
Portions made for big
appetites.
✉ 866 Broadway ☎ 415/781
7058 🕐 Lunch, dinner

Aqua (£££)
Glamorous downtown
restaurant specialising in
French-American gourmet
seafood.
✉ 252 California Street ☎
415/956 9662 🕐 Lunch, dinner

Balboa Cafe (££)
Trendy café with a traditional
American menu. The place
to 'see and be seen'.
✉ 3199 Fillmore Street ☎
415/921 3944 🕐 Lunch, dinner

Bix (££)
Martinis, cigar smoke,
upscale crowd and great
steaks and seafood make
this one of San Francisco's
most popular restaurants.
Reservations recommended.
✉ 56 Gold Street ☎ 415/433
6300 🕐 Lunch, dinner

Cafe Kati (££)
Small American restaurant
with 'arty' crowd and experi-
mental dishes. Large
portions are good value.
✉ 1963 Sutter Street
☎ 415/775 7313 🕐 Lunch,
dinner; closed Mon

Caffe Sport (££)
Family-style Italian restaurant
that is a favourite with North
Beach regulars. Sicilian
specialities.
✉ 574 Green Street
☎ 415/981 1251 🕐 Lunch,
dinner; no credit cards

Le Charm (£)
French bistro and garden
with terrific prix fixe menu.

✉ 315 5th Street ☎ 415/516
6128 🕐 Lunch, dinner

Chez Michel (£££)
French-Californian cuisine in
romantic wharf setting.
Gourmet food is pricey, but
tasty, and the service is
impeccable.
✉ 804 N Point Street ☎
415/775 7036 🕐 Lunch, dinner

La Cumbre Taqueria (£)
By far the best Mexican
restaurant in San Francisco.
No frills, but a 'can't miss'
when only a burrito will do.
✉ 515 Valencia Street ☎
415/344 8989 🕐 Lunch, dinner

Della Torre (£££)
Italian restaurant in North
Beach area that gets rave
reviews for food and
ambience. Garden seating
with view of the bay.
✉ 1349 Montgomery Street
☎ 415/296 1111 🕐 Lunch,
dinner

Dottie's True Blue Cafe (£)
Great diner for typical
American food. Home-style
atmosphere and affordable
prices make it a hit.
✉ 522 Jones Street
☎ 415/885 2767 🕐 Breakfast,
lunch, dinner

Ebisu (££)
Top-rated sushi and
traditional Asian food. Long
queues occasionally, but
worth the wait.
✉ 1283 Ninth Avenue ☎
415/566 1770 🕐 Lunch, dinner

Firefly (££)
Local favourite for home
cooking and friendly service.
A great place to people
watch.
✉ 4288 24th Street ☎
415/821 7652 🕐 Lunch, dinner

Fleur de Lys (£££)
The city's most romantic restaurant. Attentive service and superb contemporary French food.
✉ 777 Sutter Street ☎ 415/673 7779 ⏰ Lunch, dinner

Fog City Diner (£)
Upscale '50s-style diner on Telegraph Hill. American and seafood specialities.
✉ 1300 Battery Street ☎ 415/982 2000 ⏰ Lunch, dinner

The House(£)
Quaint and quiet with superb food Asian-American cuisine at a moderate price.
✉ 1230 Grant Avenue ☎ 415/986 8612 ⏰ Lunch, dinner; closed Sun, Mon

Jacks (££)
Originally opened in 1864, with turn-of-the-century furnishings and classic cuisine. Reservations recommended.
✉ 615 Sacramento Street ☎ 415/986 9854 ⏰ Lunch, dinner

Kate's Kitchen (£)
Authentic, inexpensive 'soul' food in the famous Haight-Ashbury district. Great for breakfast or late-night dining.
✉ 471 Haight Street ☎ 415/626 3984 ⏰ Breakfast, lunch, dinner; no credit cards

Lulu (££)
Innovative, Mediterranean bistro located in a large converted warehouse. Family-style service with excellent food.
✉ 816 Folsom ☎ 415/495 5775 ⏰ Lunch, dinner

The Mandarin (£££)
Long-time favourite for incredible views and exotic environment. Chinese cuisine; specialises in Peking duck.
✉ 900 N Point Street ☎ 415/673 8812 ⏰ Lunch, dinner

Mel's Drive In (£)
A revival of the popular 1950s-style drive-in. Top-rated burgers, fries and milk shakes and, of course, a great jukebox.
✉ 2165 Lombard Street ☎ 415/921 2867 ✉ 3355 Geary Street ☎ 415/387 2244 ⏰ Lunch, dinner, open late; no credit cards

One Market (£££)
American food prepared by one of the top chefs in the country.
✉ 1 Market Street ☎ 415/777 5577 ⏰ Lunch, dinner

Perry's (£)
Local watering hole, so popular with the young set that they added a second location. Good American food and comfortable ambience.
✉ 1944 Union Street ☎ 415/922 9022 ✉ 185 Sutter Street ☎ 415/989 6895 ⏰ Lunch, dinner

Plump Jack Cafe (££)
'Hot spot' specialising in American food. Offers top-notch wine list. Reservations may be difficult to get, but you'll be glad you persisted.
✉ 3127 Fillmore Street ☎ 415/563 4755 ⏰ Lunch, dinner

Swan Oyster Depot (££)
Unique seafood emporium in operation since 1912. Service from an old-fashioned marble bar.
✉ 1517 Polk Street ☎ 415/673 1101 ⏰ Lunch, dinner; no credit cards

Diversity
The strength of any great city is the diversity of its cuisine and restaurants. San Francisco certainly flexes its muscles in this respect. The most elegant restaurants are located in the centre of the city. By region, the best Italian can be found in the North Beach area, while Latin dishes are the highlights in the Mission District. Chinatown offers Asian restaurants, naturally, from Thai to Vietnamese to Cambodian.

93

Los Angeles

Ethnic Mix

Los Angeles restaurants reflect the city's diverse ethnic mix. Tail-o-the-Pup hot dog stand (San Vicente & Beverly) combines architectural uniqueness with a great dog, and just a couple of blocks away, La Cienega Boulevard's 'restaurant row' offers eateries for every taste and budget. Because smoking is prohibited in Los Angeles County restaurants and the weather is gorgeous year-round, patio dining is nouvelle vogue.

Bob Burns (££)

For great prime rib and Bloody Marys at the Santa Monica beach, this is the place. Live music nightly.

✉ 202 Wilshire ☎ 310/393 6777 🕐 Lunch, dinner

Border Grill (££)

Hip cantina by the beach. Serves exotic Mexican specialities. Stylish ambience; great margaritas.

✉ 1445 4th Street, Santa Monica ☎ 310/451 1655 🕐 Lunch, dinner

Buffalo Club (££)

Westside's newest club/ restaurant, with top-notch American cuisine.

✉ 1520 Olympic Boulevard (at 15th Street) ☎ 310/450 8600 🕐 Lunch, dinner

Cheesecake Factory (£)

One of the most popular restaurants in Southern California because of its huge portions of traditional American fare and a gauntlet of cheesecake.

✉ 364 N Beverly Drive, Beverly Hills ☎ 310/278 7270 ✉ 4142 Via Marina, Marina del Rey ☎ 310/306 3344 🕐 Lunch, dinner

Dan Tana's (££)

Long-time celebrity hangout for Italian food, the best steaks and fresh lobster. *Very* Hollywood.

✉ 9071 Santa Monica Boulevard ☎ 310/375 9444 🕐 Dinner only, but open late

Drai's (£££)

Current favourite of Hollywood elite. Pricey, but excellent French cuisine.

✉ 730 N La Cienega Boulevard ☎ 310/358 8585 🕐 Dinner; lunch Fri only

Duke's (£)

Sunset Strip coffee shop/ diner where fantastic omelettes attract the young and hip. Long queues at breakfast, especially on weekends.

✉ 8909 Sunset Boulevard ☎ 310/652 3100 🕐 Breakfast, lunch, dinner; no credit cards

Formosa Cafe (£)

Legendary cafe for enter-tainment-industry types. Continental cuisine.

✉ 7156 Santa Monica Boulevard ☎ 213/850 9050 🕐 Lunch, dinner

The Ivy (£££)

Great American food and the place to see and be seen in LA. Outdoor patio. Reservations are a must.

✉ 113 N Robertson Boulevard ☎ 310/274 8303 🕐 Lunch, dinner

Jones Hollywood (££)

Crowded, loud and very trendy, but the food is surprisingly good. Continental cuisine.

✉ 7205 Santa Monica Boulevard ☎ 213/850 1727 🕐 Lunch, dinner

Lawry's Prime Rib (£££)

The best for prime rib anywhere, supposedly, in the world. 'To die for', says one. You decide, but make reservations early.

✉ 100 N La Cienega ☎ 310/652 2827 🕐 Dinner only

Maple Drive (£££)

Well-known Beverly Hills celebrity-owned restaurant. American menu and pleasing jazz.

✉ 345 N Maple Drive, Beverly Hills ☎ 310/274 9800 🕐 Lunch, dinner; closed Sun

Mexican Village (£)
Authentic, home-style Mexican cooking by father and son of famed Oliveras family.
✉ 3668 W Beverly Boulevard ☎ 213/385 0479 🕐 Lunch, dinner

Musso and Frank (££)
A touch of 'Old Hollywood' serving traditional fare. Great martinis and the best Caesar salad in LA.
✉ 6667 Hollywood Boulevard ☎ 213/467 5123 🕐 Lunch, dinner; closed Sun, Mon

L'Orangerie (£££)
Excellent modern-classic French food that is second only to the impressive décor. Impeccable service; terrace dining. Consistently in California's top listings.
✉ 903 N La Cienega Boulevard ☎ 310/652 9770 🕐 Lunch, dinner; closed Mon

Pacific Dining Car (£££)
Downtown standard for steaks and seafood. Draws day-time business crowd but is best in the evening. Reservations recommended.
✉ 1310 W 6th Street ☎ 213/483 6000 🕐 Breakfast, lunch, dinner

Parkway Grill (££)
Parkway's Continental cuisine is worth the trip to Pasadena. Also California fare.
✉ 510 S Arroyo Parkway, Pasadena ☎ 818/795 1001 🕐 Lunch, dinner

Patina (£££)
Comfortable and unpretentious French bistro (really!).
✉ 5955 Melrose Avenue ☎ 213/467 1108 🕐 Dinner only

Roscoe's House of Chicken and Waffles (£)
Famous with locals for its informal setting, sinfully greasy chicken, and delectable waffles any time of day. Two locations. No reservations.
✉ 1514 N Gower Street ☎ 213/752 6211 ✉ 5006 W Pico ☎ 213/934 4405 🕐 Breakfast, lunch, dinner, open late

Spago (£££)
World-renowned for chef Wolfgang Puck's gourmet pizzas, and its star-studded Academy Awards party. Also fine California cuisine.
✉ 8795 Sunset Boulevard ☎ 310/652 4025 🕐 Dinner only

Tommy's (£)
Perhaps the greatest hamburger stand on the planet. Greasy, but great!
✉ 2575 Beverly Boulevard ☎ 213/389 9060 🕐 Open all the time; no credit cards

Tommy Tang's (££)
Very hip Thai restaurant. Indoor and outdoor dining.
✉ 7313 Melrose Avenue ☎ 213/937 5733 🕐 Lunch, dinner; closed Mon

Trattoria Farfalla (£)
Italian café serving great thin-crust pizzas. Usually crowded, but worth the wait.
✉ 1978 N Hillhurst Street ☎ 213/661 7365 🕐 Lunch, dinner

Valentino (£££)
Elegant, expensive Italian, with a great wine list and impeccable service. Consistently rated among the best. Reservations required.
✉ 3115 Pico Boulevard, Santa Monica ☎ 310/829 4313 🕐 Dinner; lunch only on Fri

People-watching
California was at the forefront of the coffee-house and health food restaurants craze. It is also the state where 'hanging out' and 'people-watching' have been elevated to an art form. Sunset Plaza (West Hollywood), Ventura Boulevard (San Fernando Valley), La Brea (Hollywood), Melrose Avenue (Hollywood), and the beaches in Venice, Santa Monica and Malibu are exceptional areas to go when you wish to sit, feed and watch.

San Diego

Whatever You Choose
San Diego's restaurants are known for their emphasis on seafood and South-of-the-Border cuisine. The Downtown, Old Town and Hillcrest sections offer the most diverse choices of dining and ambience. Other areas that offer cafés, coffee-houses, diners and fine dining are Ocean Beach, Point Loma, Coronado, Mission Beach and Pacific Beach. The San Diego area also has a great many health food and vegetarian restaurants.

Anthony's Star of the Sea Room (£££)
Family-owned seafood restaurant. Great service, beautiful harbour views. Jacket required.
✉ **1360 Harbor Drive** ☎ **619/232 7408** 🕐 **Lunch, dinner**

Athens Market (££)
No-frills Greek restaurant. Belly dancers on weekends.
✉ **109 W F Street** ☎ **619/232 7408** 🕐 **Lunch, dinner**

Bayou Bar and Grill (££)
Cajun casual with outdoor patio. Sunday brunch.
✉ **329 Market St** ☎ **619/696 8747** 🕐 **Lunch, dinner**

Belgian Lion (££)
Unique Belgian décor, classic French/Belgian menu.
✉ **2265 Bacon Street, Mission Bay** ☎ **619/223 2700** 🕐 **Lunch, dinner Thu–Sat only**

Cafe Lulu (£)
Coffeehouse/restaurant in the Gaslamp Quarter neigh-bourhood. One of the few late-night places to eat.
✉ **419 F Street** ☎ **619/238 0114** 🕐 **Breakfast, lunch, dinner; no credit cards**

Café Pacifica (££)
Good seafood specialities in unique, old cemetery setting.
✉ **2414 San Diego Avenue, Old Town** ☎ **619/219 6666, 619/291 6666** 🕐 **Lunch, dinner**

City Delicatessen (£)
Centrally located Jewish deli.
✉ **535 University Avenue** ☎ **619/295 2747** 🕐 **Breakfast, lunch, dinner**

Dakota (£)
Mesquite-grilled fish and fowl at very agreeable prices. Live music.
✉ **901 5th Avenue** ☎ **619/234 5554** 🕐 **Lunch, dinner**

Dick's Last Resort (£)
Continental dining in a converted warehouse.
✉ **345 5th Avenue** ☎ **619/231 9100** 🕐 **Lunch, dinner**

Le Fontainebleau (£££)
Expensive French restaurant in The Westgate Hotel. Offers gallery of original oil paintings and award-winning seafood and veal. Nightly pianist.
✉ **1055 Second Avenue** ☎ **619/238 1818** 🕐 **Lunch, dinner**

Hob Nob Hill (££)
Family-owned. Specialities are fried scallops and rack of lamb. Special kids' menu.
✉ **2271 First Avenue (near Balboa Park)** ☎ **619/239 8176** 🕐 **Lunch, dinner**

Kansas City Barbeque (£)
No-frills barbecue stand with lots of personality.
✉ **610 W Market Street** ☎ **619/231 9680** 🕐 **Lunch, dinner**

Old Town Mexican Cafe (£)
Best Mexican fare in San Diego.
✉ **2489 San Diego Avenue** ☎ **619/297 4330** 🕐 **Lunch, dinner**

Rainwaters on Ketner (£££)
Private club atmosphere with standard American cuisine. Dress code enforced.
✉ **1202 Ketner Boulevard** ☎ **619/233 5757** 🕐 **Lunch, dinner; no lunch on weekends**

Sfuzzi (££)
Patio dining with Italian specialities. Pizza straight from the wood-fired oven.
✉ **340 5th Avenue** ☎ **619/231 2323** 🕐 **Lunch, dinner**

Rest of California

Eureka
Sea Grill (££)
Extensive seafood menu that includes cod Louisiana and Hawaiian mahi-mahi.
✉ 316 'E' St, Old Town ☎ 707/443 7187 🕐 Lunch, dinner

Mendocino
Mendocino Hotel (£££)
Extremely cosy, antique-filled hotel. Dine in elegant Victorian parlour or garden café. Excellent Continental cuisine and seafood specialities.
✉ 45080 Main Street ☎ 707/937 0511 🕐 Breakfast, lunch, dinner

Montecito
Montecito Cafe (££)
Until recently, a well-kept local secret. California cuisine; warm setting in The Montecito Inn.
✉ 1295 Coast Village Road ☎ 805/969 3392 🕐 Lunch, dinner

Stonehouse (£££)
Regional cuisine in rustic, romantic setting. At the world-renowned San Ysidro Ranch Resort.
✉ 900 San Ysidro Road, Montecito ☎ 805/969 5046 🕐 Lunch, dinner

Morro Bay
Hoppes (££)
International cuisine and great wine list.
✉ 901 Embarcadero ☎ 805/772 9012 🕐 Lunch Fri–Sun, dinner; closed Tue

Ojai
Olema Farm House Restaurant (££)
This shingle-sided eatery was a stagecoach stop in 1872, but today's fare is nouveau American.
✉ 10005 Highway 1, Olema ☎ 415/663 1264 🕐 Breakfast, lunch, dinner

Suzanne's Cuisine (££)
A real gem, off the beaten path. Inexpensive California cuisine.
✉ 502 W Ojai Avenue ☎ 805/640 1961 🕐 Lunch, dinner

Wheeler Hot Springs Spa and Restaurant (££)
After a massage and dip in a hot spring, dress, then dine to the sound of live music. Great lobster and California cuisine.
✉ 16825 Maricopa Highway ☎ 805/646 8131 🕐 Lunch, dinner Tue–Sun

Orange County
Antoine (£££)
Orange County's most elegant French restaurant; quiet, with impressive décor. Located in the Sutton Place Hotel.
✉ 4500 MacArthur Boulevard, Newport Beach ☎ 714/476 2001 🕐 Dinner only

Bistango (££)
Combination of restaurant and art gallery. Offers varied Continental cuisine, prix fixe. Extensive wine list and nightly entertainment.
✉ 19100 Von Karman Avenue, Irvine ☎ 714/752 5222 🕐 Lunch, dinner

Cafe Zinc (£)
Stereotypical California, vegetarian coffee-house. Great muffins. Hangout of the arty set. Usually crowded, but well worth the wait.
✉ 350 Ocean Avenue, Laguna Beach ☎ 714/494 6302 🕐 Breakfast, lunch only

Satisfying Your Needs
Food lovers will find California like no other place on earth in its diversity and sheer number of restaurants and cafés. California has initiated such US culinary trends as sushi bars, the buzz-word nouvelle and, naturally, California cuisine. Although Mexican and South American dishes are prevalent, you can satisfy just about any food craving in the Golden State.

Ocean Views

From San Diego to the top of the state, along California Route 1, you are guaranteed to find small inns with sweeping views of the Pacific and excellent food at moderate prices. Or, for funky fun and lots of food for little money, there are also the roadhouses, like the not-to-be-missed Patrick's in Santa Monica.

Cafe Zoolu (££)

Funky and eclectic. Known for great soups, grilled specialities and vegetarian delights.

✉ 860 Glenneyre, Laguna Beach ☎ 714/494 6825 🕐 Dinner only; closed Mon, Tue

Clay Oven (£)

Delightful Indian restaurant with friendly service and great prices. Good lunch buffet.

✉ 15435 Jeffrey Road (Irvine Center), Irvine ☎ 714/552 2851 🕐 Lunch, dinner

Gustaf Anders (£££)

Scandinavian dining featuring an excellent choice of fresh seafood.

✉ 1651 Sunflower Avenue, Santa Ana ☎ 714/668 1737 🕐 Lunch, dinner

Jack Shrimp (££)

Spicy Cajun, casual environment; moderately priced.

✉ 2400 W Coast Highway, Newport Beach ☎ 714/650 5577 🕐 Lunch (Fri only), dinner

McCharles House and Tearoom (££)

Superb Continental menu. Famous for its desserts. Unique Victorian décor, pleasant patio under huge eucalyptus trees.

✉ 335 S 'C' Street, Tustin ☎ 714/731 4063 🕐 Call for opening times

Oysters (££)

New and trendy place for fresh seafood and wine from the owner's vineyard. Live entertainment.

✉ 2515 E Coast Highway, Corona del Mar ☎ 714/675 7411 🕐 Lunch, dinner

Stix (££)

Budget Chinese restaurant with fast, friendly service.

✉ 28251 Crown Valley Parkway, Laguna Niguel ☎ 714/831 7849 🕐 Lunch, dinner

Topaz Cafe (££)

Continental and South-western cuisine in the Bowers Museum.

✉ 2002 N Main Street, Santa Ana ☎ 714/835 2002 🕐 Lunch, dinner

21 Ocean Front (£££)

Charming seafood restaurant at the foot of Newport Pier.

✉ 2100 W Oceanfront, Newport Beach ☎ 714/675 2566 🕐 Dinner only

Z Bistro (£)

The astounding variety of pizzas makes this a popular spot.

✉ 361 Forrest Avenue, Laguna Beach ☎ 714/497 9444 🕐 Lunch, dinner

Zov's Bistro (££)

Trendy spot with imaginative Mediterranean cuisine and fresh bread from the on-site bakery.

✉ 1774 E 17th, Tustin ☎ 714/838 8855 🕐 Lunch, dinner; closed Tue

Palm Springs/Palm Desert

Casuelas Cafe (£)

Mexican cuisine in a 'no frills' environment that the locals flock to.

✉ 73703 Highway 111, Palm Desert ☎ 619/568 001 🕐 Lunch, dinner

Cedar Creek Inn (££)

Home-town favourite for reliable American food.

✉ 1555 S Palm Canyon Drive ☎ 619/325 7300 ✉ 73445 El

Paseo, Palm Desert ☎ 619/340
1236 🕐 Lunch, dinner

Cuistot (£££)
Popular and elegant
California-French. Specialities
are veal and rack of lamb.
Pricey but worth it.
✉ 7311 El Paseo, Palm Desert
☎ 619/340 1000 🕐 Lunch,
dinner; closed Mon

John Henry's Cafe (££)
Bargain spot for large
portions of great American
food and superb desserts.
✉ 1785 E Tahquitz Canyon
Way, Palm Springs ☎ 619/327
7667 🕐 Dinner only; closed
Sun

Otani Garden (££)
Japanese dining featuring
respectful service and
wonderful Sunday brunch.
✉ 1000 Tahquitz Canyon Way,
Palm Springs ☎ 619/327 6700
🕐 Lunch, dinner

San Luis Obispo
Big Sky Cafe (£)
Caribbean cuisine in a fun
and casual environment.
✉ 1121 Broad Street ☎
805/545 5401 🕐 Lunch, dinner

Buono Tavola (££)
Great-value Italian restaurant
in a casual, country setting.
✉ 1121 Broad Street ☎
805/545 8000 🕐 Lunch, dinner;
closed Sun

Santa Barbara
The Bakery (£)
Wonderful, fresh-baked
pastry and breads.
✉ 129 E Anapumu ☎ 805/962
2089 🕐 Breakfast, lunch,
dinner

The Ballard Store (££)
Affordable prix fixe
Continental menu.

✉ 2449 Baseline Avenue
☎ 805/688 5319 🕐 Lunch,
dinner; closed Mon

**Brophy Brother's Clam Bar
and Restaurant (££)**
Spectacular views and an
energetic crowd.
✉ 721 Harbor Way ☎
805/966 4418 🕐 Lunch, dinner

Carlito's Cafe (£)
Budget Mexican and
interesting vegetarian plates.
✉ 1324 State Street ☎
805/962 7117 🕐 Lunch, dinner

The Hitching Post (£)
Barbecue, steaks and french
fries in a casual roadhouse
atmosphere.
✉ 406 E Highway 246, Buellton
☎ 805/688 0676 ✉ 3325 Point
Sal Road, Casmalia ☎ 805/937
6151 🕐 Lunch, dinner

Wine Country
Bistro Don Giovanni (££)
Serves Italian and
Mediterranean specialities in
a beautiful artistic setting.
Daily pasta specials.
✉ 4110 St Helena Highway,
Napa ☎ 707/224 3300 🕐
Lunch, dinner

**East Side Oyster Bar &
Grill (££)**
One of the best and most
innovative restaurants in
Northern California serving
California cuisine.
✉ 133 E Napa Street, Sonoma
☎ 707/939 1266 🕐 Lunch,
dinner

Mustards (££)
Napa Valley's trendiest and
most popular spot for
California cuisine.
Reservations recommended.
✉ 7399 St Helena Highway,
St Helena ☎ 707/944 2424
🕐 Lunch, dinner

Roadside Stands
To compliment California's
wide range of restaurants
and cuisines, an
abundance of roadside
stands offer fresh-picked
produce and fruit. There is
no better way to sample
the culinary diversity of a
region, and whether you
want a refreshing and
healthy travelling snack or
an inexpensive breakfast
to enjoy in your room,
you'll find these roadside
wares excellent value.

San Francisco

Prices
You may expect to pay the following prices per room per night.

£ = under $50
££ = between $50 and $125
£££ = over $125

Luxury Hotels
In California, you can find just about any type of lodging. In the large cities, European and Mediterranean styles dominate the luxury hotels. There are many landmark hotels and inns in the state, and many more that have incredible views and amenities. Expect centrally located urban areas to be the most expensive. In San Francisco's financial district, Nob Hill, you'll find refurbished and updated turn-of-the-century grand hotels.

Archbishop's Mansion (££)
Historic 1904 bed-and-breakfast with stained-glass windows and elegant European furnishings.
✉ 335 Powell Street
☎ 415/641 0188

Beresford Arms Hotel (££)
A traditional hotel with Continental breakfast. Tea, wine and snacks in the afternoon. Near Union Square.
✉ 701 Post Street ☎ 415/673 2600 ♿ Wheelchair access

Comfort Inn by the Bay (£)
Near Lombard Street and the major attractions. Reasonable rates.
✉ 2775 Van Ness Avenue
☎ 415/928 5000
♿ Wheelchair access

The Fairmont Hotel and Tower (£££)
Newly renovated historic hotel, situated atop Nob Hill.
✉ 950 Mason Street
☎ 415/772 5000
♿ Wheelchair access

Four Season's Clift (£££)
This art deco hotel is one of the city's most famous. Oriental carpets, chandeliers and tastefully decorated rooms.
✉ 495 Geary Street
☎ 415/775 4700

Hotel Triton (££)
Near Chinatown. Tasteful art deco design with exhibitions of local artwork in the lobby.
✉ 342 Grant Avenue
☎ 415/394 0500
♿ Wheelchair access

The Inn at the Opera (£££)
Near Performing Arts Center. Small and elegant with first-rate service.
✉ 333 Fulton Street
☎ 415/863 8400
♿ Wheelchair access

The Inn San Francisco (££)
An 1872 Italian mansion in the Mission District.
✉ 943 S Van Ness ☎ 415/641 0188

Majestic Hotel (£££)
Restored Edwardian hotel, dating to 1902.
✉ 1500 Sutter Street
☎ 415/441 1100
♿ Wheelchair access

Mark Hopkins Inter-Continental (£££)
On the site of the old Mark Hopkins mansion. Offers a spectacular view of the city.
✉ 1 Nob Hill ☎ 415/392 3434

Mill Valley Inn (££)
Beautiful stucco hotel at the centre of this small, artistic community.
✉ 165 Throckmorton Avenue, Mill Valley ☎ 415/389 6608

Queen Anne (£)
Converted Victorian house, impressive for its art deco style. Complimentary breakfast, and afternoon tea and sherry; attentive staff.
✉ 1590 Sutter Street
☎ 415/441 2828
♿ Wheelchair access

Sir Francis Drake (££)
Opulence with bed-and-breakfast flavour.
✉ 450 Powell Street
☎ 415/392 7755

York Hotel (££)
Renovated 1922 hotel with marble floors. Parts of Alfred Hitchcock's *Vertigo* were filmed here.
✉ 940 Sutter Street
☎ 415/885 6800

Los Angeles

The Argyle (£££)
An LA landmark; 15 stories of art deco elegance at the end of Sunset Strip. Popular movie location.
✉ 8358 Sunset Boulevard, W Hollywood ☎ 213/654 7100

Beverly Hills Hotel (£££)
This 1912 landmark was restored in the early 1990s by its owner, the Sultan of Brunei. Famous for its private bungalows and the celebrity-packed Polo Lounge.
✉ 9641 Sunset Boulevard ☎ 310/281 2905

Chateau Marmont Hotel (££)
Favourite of film and music communities in the style of a Loire Valley château.
✉ 8221 Sunset Boulevard ☎ 213/656 1010

Holiday Inn (££)
Reliable accommodation from this international chain.
✉ 1020 S Fiqueroa St, Downtown LA ☎ 213/748 1291

Hollywood Roosevelt (££)
Site of first Academy Awards presentation (1927). Centrally located (▶ 21).
✉ 7000 Hollywood Boulevard ☎ 213/462 8056

Hotel Bel Air (£££)
Most exotic of all LA hotels. A favourite hideaway for the rich and famous. Mediterranean décor.
✉ 701 Stone Canyon Road ☎ 310/472 1211

Malibu Beach Inn (££)
Mediterranean-style hotel on a white-sand shore.
✉ 22878 Pacific Coast Highway, Malibu ☎ 310/456 6444

New Otani Hotel and Garden (£££)
Japanese-style hotel in downtown LA. Beautiful gardens and well-appointed rooms.
✉ 120 S Los Angeles Street ☎ 213/629 1200

Sheraton Universal (£££)
Views of Hollywood Hills and San Fernando Valley. Walking distance to Universal City attractions. Good-value weekend packages.
✉ 333 Universal Terrace Parkway ☎ 818/980 1212

Shutters on the Beach (£££)
Contemporary beachfront hotel with all the amenities. Marble bathrooms, sweeping ocean views.
✉ 1 Pico Boulevard, Santa Monica ☎ 310/459 0300

Sofitel Ma Maison (££)
Mediterranean-style hotel with affordable rates. Across from the Beverly Center Mall (▶ 107).
✉ 8555 Beverly Boulevard ☎ 310/278 5444

Sunset Marquis (£££)
Mediterranean décor, mostly suites. Set on a residential street, the Marquis is a favourite of the entertainment community for its casual, comfortable atmosphere.
✉ 1200 N Alta Loma ☎ 310/657 4000

Wyndham Bel Age (£££)
All-suite hotel in the heart of West Hollywood. Roof-top swimming pool with fantastic views of the city.
✉ 1020 N San Vicente ☎ 310/854 1111

Convenient Location
In Los Angeles, the Westside hotels (from Hollywood to Santa Monica) are probably the best locations for those who wish to visit LA's attractions and enjoy the sights. For the best rates, inquire at the specific hotels for package deals, or call one of the many 'brokers' that are emerging in the hotel industry (check local listings for names and numbers).

San Diego/Rest of California

Beside the Sea

The San Diego area is a great place to book into a beachside hotel or resort. The pleasing year-round climate will make it almost irresistible to spend an afternoon by the pool or at the beach. La Jolla, Del Mar and Laguna Beach are just a few areas to look into for a time of rest and relaxation in the sun. Even though winter temperatures are still nearly perfect, many hotels and inns reduce their rates.

San Diego

Bay Club Marina and Inn (£££)

Large rooms, some with private balconies and patios. On the Marina.

✉ 2131 Shelter Island Drive
☎ 619/224 8888

Clarion Bayview (££)

Located in the Gaslamp Quarter, close to main attractions. Views of bay and downtown.

✉ 660 'K' Street ☎ 619/696 0234

Horton Grand (£££)

The oldest building in San Diego (1886). Victorian décor with impressive lobby.

✉ 311 Island Avenue
☎ 619/544 1886

Hotel del Coronado (£££)

Famous Victorian hotel from 1880s, jutting out into the bay. Large rooms, some suites. One room is 'haunted'.

✉ 1500 Orange Avenue
☎ 619/435 6611

Humphrey's Half Moon Inn (££)

Beautiful gardens and island décor overlooking the Bay.

✉ 2303 Shelter Island Drive
☎ 619/224 3411

La Costa Resort and Spa (£££)

Large, luxury resort with golf, tennis and watersports.

✉ 2100 Costa Del Mar Road, Carlsbad ☎ 619/438 9111

Le Meridien San Diego at Coronado (£££)

French and Californian décor on 16 acres of exotically landscaped grounds.

✉ 2000 Second Street
☎ 619/435 3000

Travel Lodge Harbor Island (£)

Affordable rates near the airport.

✉ 1960 Harbor Island Drive
☎ 619/291 6700

The Westgate (£££)

Modern luxury in downtown tower. Many rooms with harbour views. Close to Horton Plaza.

✉ 1055 Second Avenue
☎ 619/238 1818

The Rest of California

Big Bear Lake

Goldmine Lodge (£)

Small lodge with affordable units situated in the pine forest region of Big Bear Lake.

✉ 42268 Moonridge Road
☎ 909/866 8786

Big Sur

Ventana Inn (£££)

Luxurious hideaway, comprises 59 separate bungalows. Sweeping views of the coastline.

✉ California Highway 1
☎ 408/667 2331

Carmel

Mission Ranch (££)

Former dairy farm saved from destruction by actor Clint Eastwood. Rustic comfort.

✉ 26270 Dolores Street
☎ 408/624 6436

Tickle Pink Inn at Carmel Highlands (£££)

Coastline views from secluded cottages and rooms. Nonchalant luxury. Afternoon wine and cheese service.

✉ 155 Highlands Drive
☎ 408/624 1244

Catalina Island
Hotel Metropole (££)
Magnificent ocean views from the rooftop sun deck and spa. In Metropole Marketplace.
✉ **205 Crescent Avenue, Avalon** ☎ **310/510 1884**

Hotel Vista Del Mar (££)
Resort hotel overlooking beach with larger, comfortable rooms; most with spectacular views.
✉ **417 Crescent Avenue, Avalon** ☎ **310/510 1452**

Death Valley
Furnace Creek Inn (£££)
Native American décor, built in the 1920s. Choose between regular motel-style rooms and furnished cabins.
✉ **About 1 mile south on CA 190** ☎ **760/786 2361**
🕐 **Oct–May only**

Eureka
Best Western Thunderbird Inn (£)
Comfortable lodging near Humboldt State Park.
✉ **232 W 5th Street** ☎ **707/443 2234**

Half Moon Bay
The Beach House (££)
Large rooms with spectacular ocean views, fireplaces like an old New England summer home. Jacuzzis, saunas.
✉ **6 miles north of Half Moon Bay** ☎ **415/712 0220**

Lake Arrowhead
Lake Arrowhead Resort (££)
On the lake in Arrowhead Village. All rooms face the lakefront. Fishing, boating, children's activities.
✉ **Arrowhead Village, Box 1699** ☎ **909/336 1511**

Lake Tahoe
Best Western Station House Inn (££)
Central to the lake, with great sporting activities. Just a short hop to the border casinos.
✉ **901 Park Avenue, South Lake Tahoe** ☎ **916/542 1101**

Mammoth Lakes
Mammoth Mountain Inn (£££)
Resort complex; free transportation to the ski areas. Horseback riding and hiking/hunting trails are on offer.
✉ **1 Minaret Road** ☎ **619/934 2581**

Mendocino
Harbor House Inn (££)
Small hotel filled with antiques and original artworks.
✉ **5600 S CA Highway 1** ☎ **707/877 3203**

Monterey
Old Monterey Inn (£££)
English country hotel boasting acres of gardens and spectacular views of Monterey Bay.
✉ **500 Martin Street** ☎ **408/375 8284**

Morro Bay
Best Western El Rancho (£)
Unique redwood lobby. Very reasonable rates.
✉ **2460 Main Street** ☎ **805/772 2212**

Mount Shasta
Treehouse Best Western (££)
Terrific views of the mountain and excellent skiing in the winter.
✉ **Lake Street just off the I–5** ☎ **530/926 3101**

Bed and Breakfast
A recent trend in lodging is the popularity of the bed and breakfast and the country inn. Many of these are found in Northern California and Wine Country regions. Many of those who live in the major cities look forward to a weekend in the country at one of these small inns (usually only 10 to 20 rooms). Reservations are difficult to get on the weekends and in the summer, so book well in advance.

Motels
For those on a tight budget, it's possible to find a decent motel room (double occupancy) for under $50. Most offer in-room phones, cable television and a pool. There are many motel 'chains' that offer safe, clean, reasonably priced lodging for those in transit. Some to look for are Motel 6, Econolodge and Quality Inn.

Ojai
Ojai Valley Inn (£££)
Plush rural setting with championship golf course. Set in 220 acres.
✉ Country Club Road
☎ 805/646 5511

Orange County
Four Seasons Hotel (£££)
One of the finest hotels in the state. Contemporary design with tree-lined swimming pool and tennis courts.
✉ 690 Newport Center Drive, Newport Beach ☎ 714/759 0808

Hotel Laguna (£)
A hotel with a history. Affordable and funky, with private beach for guests
✉ 425 S Coast Highway, Laguna Beach ☎ 714/494 1151

Surf and Sand Hotel (££)
Tasteful, elegant hotel on the beach, near the galleries, shops and restaurants. All rooms with ocean views.
✉ 1555 S Coast Highway, Laguna Beach ☎ 714/497 4477

Waterfront Hilton Beach Resort (£££)
Large resort with beach access, watersports, dining and shopping. All rooms with ocean views.
✉ 21100 Pacific Coast Highway, Huntington Beach ☎ 714/960 7873

Palm Springs
Estrella Inn (££)
Old World inn where the charm doesn't cost extra.
✉ 415 S Belardo ☎ 760/320 4117

Marriott's Desert Springs Resort and Spa (£££)
Marriott's landmark hotel features an atrium lobby, beautifully landscaped gardens, Bob Hope Cultural Center, golf, tennis, man-made beach, an exclusive mall and canopied lagoon boats.
✉ 74855 Country Club Drive, Palm Desert ☎ 760/341 2211

Sundance Villas (£££)
Exquisite private villas for those who want to get away in style.
✉ 303 W Cabrillo Road ☎ 760/325 3888

Two Bunch Palms Inn (£££)
Secluded cottages on 300 acres. Natural hot springs, a lake and wooded walking paths.
✉ 67425 Two Bunch Palms Trail, Desert Hot Springs ☎ 760/329 8791

Pebble Beach
The Lodge at Pebble Beach (£££)
The epitome of opulence. Overlooks Carmel Bay and the world-famous Pebble Beach golf course.
✉ 3 miles north of Carmel on Highway 1 ☎ 408/624 3811

Pismo Beach
Sea Gypsy (£)
Affordable lodging on the beach.
✉ 1020 Cypress ☎ 805/773 1801

Redwood Forest
Benbow Inn (£££)
Lakeside Tudor mansion built in 1926.
✉ 445 Lake Benbow Drive, Garberville ☎ 707/923 2124
🚫 Closed Jan–Mar

Sacramento
Vizcaya (£££)
Victorian house with gazebo

and gardens. Italian marble bathrooms.
✉ 2019 21st Street
☎ 916/455 5243

San Luis Obispo
Apple Farm Inn (££)
Quaint inn with working millhouse and bakery.
✉ 2015 Monterey Street
☎ 805/544 2040

Santa Barbara
El Encanto Hotel and Garden Villas (££)
Cottages and suites with ocean views.
✉ 1900 Lausen Road
☎ 805/687 5000

Montecito Inn (£££)
Built in 1928 by Charlie Chaplin and Fatty Arbuckle, the inn takes its facilities and service quite seriously.
✉ 1295 Coast Village Road
☎ 805/969 7854

Santa Cruz
Inn at Depot Hill (£££)
A turn-of-the-century railroad depot, now pure posh.
✉ 250 Monterey Avenue
☎ 408/462 3376

Sea and Sand Inn (£)
Budget hotel, overlooking the cliffs.
✉ 201 W Cliff Drive
☎ 408/427 3400

Solvang
Solvang Royal Scandinavian Inn (££)
Tastefully decorated in original Scandinavian style. Centrally located for Solvang's attractions.
✉ 400 Alisal Road ☎ 805/688 8000

Windmill Motor Inn (££)
Unique Danish architecture at reasonable rates.

✉ 114 East Highway 246, Buellton, Solvang exit off freeway ☎ 805/688 8448

Wine Country
Auberge De Soleil (£££)
Mediterranean luxury in a Napa Valley olive grove.
✉ 180 Rutherford Hill Road, St Helena ☎ 707/963 1211

Beazley House Inn (££)
Small, turn-of-the-century home with 11 rooms, this was the first Napa B&B. Beautiful lawns and gardens.
✉ 1910 1st Street, Napa
☎ 707/257 1649

Foothill House (£££)
Charmingly remodelled, turn-of-the-century farmhouse.
✉ 3037 Foothill Boulevard, Calistoga ☎ 707/942 6933

Silverado Resort (£££)
Large resort with wine tastings and sporting facilities.
✉ 1600 Atlas Peak Road
☎ 707/257 0200

Sonoma Mission Inn and Spa (£££)
Exclusive spa in the Spanish-mission style.
✉ Sonoma Highway, Sonoma
☎ 707/938 9000

Trojan Horse Inn (££)
Very intimate. Only six rooms in this restored frontier home.
✉ 19455 Sonoma Highway, Sonoma ☎ 707/996 2430

Yosemite
Tenaya Lodge at Yosemite (££)
Rustic elegance on the river. Cookouts and wagon rides.
✉ 2 miles south of the park's south gate ☎ 209/683 6555

Campgrounds
An alternative to hotels and motels are the state's many campgrounds. Most of the state and national parks have campgrounds that offer tent or RV sites, outdoor cooking areas, public rest rooms and shower facilities. The fee is usually under $10 per night. Private campgrounds adjacent to the parks offer additional facilities at a slightly higher rate. June through September is a busy time.

Art & Antiques/ Fashion/Crafts/Stores

Popular Shopping Venues

San Francisco and Los Angeles are the two most popular shopping areas in California. From large, multi-level shopping centres to streets filled with discount and speciality shops, you can find just about anything your heart desires. Included here are just a few of the most popular areas to get you started. Check the local newspapers, especially on Sunday, for sales and discounts.

Art & Antiques

San Francisco
Fillmore Street
Speciality shops include book and music stores, and clothing from retro to new fashion.
✉ Jackson & Sutter

The Japan Center
Art galleries and Oriental gift shops, interspersed with sushi bars and tea houses.
✉ Bounded by Laguna, Geary, Fillmore, Sutter and Post streets

Los Angeles
La Cienega Boulevard south of Santa Monica Boulevard, Beverly Boulevard west of the Beverly Center, Melrose Avenue in Hollywood, and Santa Monica's Third Street Promenade are all lined with excellent, but costly antique stores and art galleries.

San Diego
Antique Row
Over 20 dealers give this street its name.
✉ Adams Avenue, Kensington

The Olde Cracker Factory
Antiques centre of the area.
✉ 448 W Market   ☎ 619/233 1669

Rest Of California

Mendocino
This small town in northern California is considered the artistic centre of the North Coast.

Mendocino Arts Center
Two art galleries, along with numerous arts and crafts fairs.
✉ 45200 Little Lake Street   ☎ 707/937 5818

Santa Rosa (Wine Country)
Railroad Square
A historic square featuring antiques stores, curio shops and restaurants.
☎ 707/569 9496

Fashion

San Francisco
Haight Street
Famous for hippies in the 1960s; some 'flower power' still remains in shops selling offbeat, vintage clothes. Great new and used book and music shops.
✉ At Ashbury Street

SoMa
Popular for bargain stores, night-spots and cafés.
✉ South of Market Street

Union Street and Square
Up-market. Large department stores are Macy's, Neiman-Marcus and Saks Fifth Avenue.
✉ Between Gough and Steiner
☎ Macy's 415/397 333;
Neiman-Marcus 415/362 3900;
Saks Fifth Avenue 415/986 4300

Los Angeles
Garment District
Fashion bargains in open store fronts and inside the huge Cooper Building. Stroll through the California Mart to see upcoming fashions.
✉ Los Angeles Street and 7th Street, Downtown

Melrose Avenue
This three-mile strip of boutiques will satisfy any taste and budget, from Aardvark's used clothing, to vintage stores and up-market boutiques.
✉ Between Highland and Doheny, Hollywood

Rodeo Drive
Renowned as being the most exclusive and expensive shopping area on the West Coast. Top designer clothes and accessories.
✉ **Between Santa Monica and Wilshire boulevards, Beverly Hills**

Venice Beach
Unique and amazingly inexpensive sunwear and hip formal dress.
✉ **Oceanfront Walk, Venice**

San Diego
The Paladion
Posh centre with Cartier, Tiffany's, Gucci and more.
✉ **Across from Horton Plaza**

Rest of California

Palm Springs
El Paseo
Two miles of exclusive shops that rival Beverly Hills Rodeo Drive. Art galleries.
✉ **Visitors Center, 2781 N Palm Canyon Drive** ☎ **760/778 8418**

Crafts

San Francisco
Fisherman's Wharf
There are four shopping centres here – Pier 39, The Cannery, Ghirardelli Square and The Anchorage.
✉ **Columbus on the Bay**

Los Angeles
Olvera Street
Mexican crafts and gifts, clothing and cafés on LA's oldest street.
✉ **Los Angeles Street**

San Diego
Gaslamp Quarter
A must for the arts and crafts crowd. Quarter encompasses 38 acres in the National Historic District.
✉ **Fifth Avenue from Broadway to the waterfront**

Stores

San Francisco
The Embarcadero Center
Shops, restaurants, offices, hotels in a huge downtown complex.
✉ **Sacramento and Clay streets** 🚇 **BART, Muni**

Ghirardelli Square
Formerly a chocolate factory, this area has become a chic centre of stores and top restaurants.
✉ **At Fisherman's Wharf**

Los Angeles
Beverly Center
Three-tiered upscale mall, with exterior elevators that offer a great view of the area. Macy's, Broadway, Bullocks, Hard Rock Café.
✉ **Beverly Boulevard and La Cienega, Beverly Hills**

Century City
Features international food court with indoor/outdoor dining, theatre, fine dining, Broadway, Bullocks.
✉ **10250 Santa Monica Boulevard, Beverly Hills**

Westside Pavilion
Multi-level with modern, open-air atrium; Nordstrom, Robinsons-May and others.
✉ **Pico and Westwood boulevards**

San Diego
Fashion Valley Mall
This and Mission Valley are the city's two main shopping centres. Six major department stores.
✉ **352 Fashion Valley Road**

Tijuana
Shoppers in San Diego often find themselves drawn to Tijuana, just across the California–Mexico border. The Free-Port status makes for great bargains. Prices are reasonable, and haggling is welcomed as part of the fun. The best shopping areas are the mall at Agua Caliente Race Track and the Avenida Revolución, the city's oldest tourist shopping area. Take precautions with your valuables when travelling across the border.

Factory Outlets/ Produce/Gifts

Outlet and Factory Stores

The latest US shopping trend is outlet and factory stores. Don't be fooled by these 'malls', however, as many of the shops rival the parent stores in pricing. Although you have to look carefully, there are enough bargains on the name-brand items to warrant the outlets' popularity. Along the same lines are huge indoor and outdoor flea markets and 'swap meets' which offer both new and used items.

Rest of California

Monterey
Cannery Row
Unique shops and restaurants line this nautical area, made famous by John Steinbeck's novel *Cannery Row*.
✉ Fisherman's Wharf

Orange County
South Coast Plaza
Orange County's largest and most exclusive mall, with three huge sections connected by free tram. All major department stores are located within this complex. Also a wide variety of speciality stores.

Rizzoli's International Bookstore
✉ Bristol & Sunflower, Costa Mesa

Factory Outlets

Folsom
Folsom Factory Store
The 50 stores include Nike, Jones NY, Bass.
✉ 13000 Folsom

Gilroy
Outlets at Gilroy
Over 100 stores. Includes The Gap, Ann Taylor, Espirit.
✉ 681 Leavesley

Lake Elsinore
Lake Elsinore Outlet Center
Van Huesen and Levi's are just two of the 100 stores.
✉ 17600 Collier Avenue

Mammoth Lakes
Mammoth Factory Store
Only 10 stores, but some of the best, like Polo, Ralph Lauren, Bass.
✉ 3343 Main Street

Monterey
American Tin Cannery Factory Outlet
Anne Klein and Joan and David are just two of the 50 stores.
✉ 125 Ocean View Boulevard, Pacific Grove

Petaluma
Petaluma Village Factory Outlet
Fifty stores from Saks to Levi's.
✉ 2200 Petaluma Boulevard

Pismo Beach
Pismo Beach Outlet Center
London Fog, Bass, Mikasa, Levi's; 40 shops in all.
✉ 333 5-Cities Drive

Solvang
Solvang Outlet Stores
Small but élite, featuring Donna Karen, Ellen Tracy, Brooks Bros.
✉ 3202 N Alisal Road

Wine Country
Napa Factory Store
Liz Claiborne, J Crew, Espirit; 50 in all.
✉ 629 Factory Street Drive, Napa

Produce

San Francisco
Chinatown
Almost as fun as finding unique produce and great bargains is watching the locals wrangle for better prices.
✉ Bordered by Broadway, Bush, Kearny and Powell streets

Los Angeles
Farmers Market
Over 100 sellers of not only fresh produce but gifts, food and clothes, all at affordable

prices. Open-air cafés
(▶ 49).
☒ **Third and Fairfax, Hollywood**

Gifts

San Francisco
Chinatown
Asian speciality shops, fresh produce, and incredible architecture (▶ 35).
☒ **Bordered by Broadway, Bush, Kearny & Powell streets**

Fisherman's Wharf
Street performers entertain as you explore the 100 shops and restaurants clustered around the piers (▶ 36).
☒ **Between The Embarcadero and Columbus Avenue**

Los Angeles
Hollywood Boulevard
The place to go to find rare movie memorabilia and posters. Theatres and restaurants for every mood and budget.
☒ **Between La Brea and Highland**

Little Tokyo
Unusual Oriental items. Outdoor shopping/dining.
☒ **San Pedro & First streets, Downtown**

Venice Beach
Outdoor booths with great prices, if you aren't distracted by the street artists and Muscle Beach iron-pumpers.
☒ **Oceanfront between Washington & Santa Monica Boulevards**

San Diego
Old Town
Small gift boutiques and cafés among flower gardens, fountains and courtyards in the style of a Mexican marketplace. One of the best antique shopping areas in Southern California. Bargain prices for valuable items at local antiques shops.
☒ **Mason Street and San Diego Avenue**

Rest of California

Monterey Bay
Peter Rabbit and Friends
Toys, music boxes and clothing featuring some of the characters and scenes from Beatrix Potter's children's stories.
☒ **Lincoln Avenue between 7th and Ocean avenues**
☎ **408/624 6854**

Sacramento
David Berkeley's
Eclectic variations from extensive wine selections by White House wine consultant, David Berkeley, to Epicurean European foods and country-flavoured gifts.
☒ **515 Pavillions Lane**
☎ **916/929 4422**

Wine Country
All Seasons Cafe Wine Shop
A selection of the best of the hundreds of wine shops in Napa Valley. Most sell gifts and other unique products, and will ship anywhere in the world.
☒ **1400 Lincoln Avenue, Calistoga** ☎ **707/942 9111**

Shaker Shops West
Quality reproductions of Shaker furniture and gifts, deep in California's north country.
☒ **5 Inverness Way, Inverness**
☎ **415/669 7256**

Farmers' Markets
Almost every city and town in California has an open-air or farmers' market, and roadside stands dot country roads and state highways. These markets are great places to find unique gifts or cherished mementoes of your visit, and their prices are generally lower than more urban retailers. Whatever type of shopping you prefer, locals residents are happy to point you to the most popular shopping places.

Children's Attractions

Avoid the Queues
Most of the larger California cities have fine museums that are inexpensive and provide interactive exhibits. A hint for avoiding long queues at theme parks is to arrive early, or just an hour or two before closing.

San Francisco
Children's Fairyland
This inexpensive park, with exhibits from nursery rhymes, is said to have intrigued Walt Disney so much he built Disneyland to duplicate it.
✉ **Grand Avenue at Park View Terrace, Oakland**
☎ **510/238 6876** 🕐 **Fri–Sun 10–4:30**

Paramount's Great America
The Bay area's place for roller coasters and other daredevil rides. Fort-Fun is an interactive parent/child area. Top Gun and Smurf Woods rides are the most popular. Also features stage shows, musicals, puppet shows and wildlife shows.
✉ **Great American Parkway, Santa Clara (about 45 miles south of San Francisco)**
☎ **408/988 1776** 🕐 **Daily 10am–11pm**

Raging Waters
The Bay area's only water theme park, with large and long waterslides designed to please. There are over 30 different attractions. Older children will love the innertube rides.
✉ **Lake Cunningham Park, San Jose** ☎ **408/270 8000**
🕐 **May–Oct, daily 10–8**

Santa Cruz Beach Boardwalk
This historical landmark, dating to 1907, was the first full-scale amusement park on the West Coast. With roller-coasters and haunted castles, bumper cars and a ferris wheel, this is an 'oldie but goodie'.
✉ **400 Beach Street, Santa Cruz** ☎ **408/426 7433**

Los Angeles
Disneyland (► 18)

Hollywood Guinness World of Records
Trivia galore from The-Animal-with-The-Smallest-Brain-in-Proportion-to-Body-Size (a Stegosaurus) to The Most Biographed Female (Marilyn Monroe).
✉ **6764 Hollywood Boulevard, Hollywood** ☎ **213/463 6433**
🕐 **Daily 10–midnight**
💰 **Moderate**

Hollywood Wax Museum (► 51)

Knott's Berry Farm (► 78)

The Pacific Ocean
For the price of petrol, the whole family can frolic on one of the many beaches that line the Pacific Ocean. Venice offers bike, skateboard and stroller rentals and playgrounds; the Pier at Santa Monica has rides, including the indoor carousel seen in the movie *The Sting*, arcades and shops; Malibu Beach is home to many celebrities. Further north on Pacific Coast Highway are more sandy beaches for sunning, swimming and surfing (like Leo Carillo, Zuma, Monterey Presidio), and there are even campgrounds right on the beach for a minimum cost. Summer reservations a must.

Universal Studios (► 54)

San Diego
Balboa Park (► 16)

Children's Museum of San Diego
Rotating interactive exhibits,

with a special emphasis on developing artistic potential in children.

📧 **200 W Island Avenue**
☎ **619/233 8792** 🕐 **Tue–Sat 10–4:30, Sun 11–4:30** 🖐 **Cheap**

San Diego Zoo (▶ 16)
☎ **619/234 3153** 🕐 **Winter, daily 9–4; summer, daily 9–9**
🖐 **Cheap**

Sea World (▶ 64)

Rest of California

La Habra
Children's Museum at La Habra
Restored railroad station exhibiting a wide range of scientific and historical artefacts. Special events and programmes.

📧 **301 Euclid Street, La Habra**
☎ **310/905 9793** 🕐 **Mon–Sat 10–5, Sun 1–5** 🖐 **Cheap**

Lake Arrowhead
Lake Arrowhead Children's Museum
Contains historical information on the area and anthropological exhibitions. Kids can experience being handicapped.

📧 **Lake Arrowhead Village**
☎ **909/336 3093** 🕐 **Daily 10–5**
🖐 **Cheap**

Paso Robles
Atascadero Lake Park and Charles Paddock Zoo
Intimate zoo with jaguars from Brazil, Bengal tigers, pink flamingos and lots of chimps. Nominal entry fee. Next to the zoo is a beautiful lake with picnic facilities.

📧 **State Route 41, south of Paso Robles** ☎ **805/461 5080**
🕐 **Zoo: Mon–Thu 10–4, Fri–Sun 10–5. Lake Park: daily until sundown**

Lake Nacimiento Resort
One of the most popular family resorts in the state. Great outdoor activities, including fishing and diving. Features a full-service marina and dock where you can rent anything from jet-skis to pontoon boats. Lodge, campgrounds, general store and RV facilities.

📧 **County Road G–14 out of Paso Robles** ☎ **805/238 3256**
🕐 **Daily to sundown**

Sacramento
Waterworld USA
Open late May to early September, this park has some of the best high-speed slides and other water attractions.

📧 **Exposition Boulevard** ☎ **916/924 0556** 🕐 **Daily 10–8**

Santa Ana
Kidseum
Kids won't even realise they're being educated about the world's many cultures as they participate in the story-telling, puppet shows and other exhibits at this inter-active museum.

📧 **1802 Main Street**
☎ **714/567 3600 (Bowes Museum and College of Art)**
🕐 **Tue–Sat 10–4, Wed until 9**

Valencia
Six Flags Magic Mountain
Specialising in thrill rides, the park also offers a mini-zoo and the Wizard's Village for the younger tots. Admission price covers everything but food, including puppet shows, dance revues and other live entertainment.

📧 **26101 Magic Mountain Parkway, off Golden State Freeway, ½ hour north of Hollywood** ☎ **805/255 4111**
🕐 **Daily 10–6**

Pacifying the Kids
For enjoyable travel with children, don't overdo it. Adult stress reflects in youngsters. Kids love to help plan excursions and navigate from the map, and allowing them to do so teaches valuable skills. To avoid grouchy kids and frazzled adults, take frequent breaks, especially on long road trips. And most importantly, see the sights through their eyes for a unique perspective often lost in the grown-up world.

Museums/Concert Halls/Nightlife

TV and Film
California's film industry means major cities teem with movie theatres. Check local papers for listings or pick up a free *LA* or *San Francisco Weekly* at restaurants, shops. For variation, there's the Silent Movie theatre (Hollywood), the alternative Red Vic Movie House (Haight), the live vaudevillian Fabulous Palm Springs Follies (☎ 619/327 0225), or join a television studio audience (☎ 818/506 0043).

Museums

San Francisco
Exploratorium/Palace of Fine Arts
Crème de la crème of science museums. Exhibits of art, science and human perception. The Tactile Dome is wonderful.
✉ 3601 Lyon Street
☎ 510/561 0360 🕐 Tue–Sun 10–5 , Wed 10–9:30, Mon, hols 10–5; Memorial Day–Labor Day daily 10–6, to 9:30 Wed

SFMOMA (► 39)
✉ 151 Third Street ☎ 510/357 4000 🕐 Tue–Sun 11–6, Thu until 9; closed Mon, major hols ✋ Free 1st Tue of month

Los Angeles
Armand Hammer Museum of Art and Cultural Center
Holds the largest US collection of French artist Honoré Dumier.
✉ 10899 Wilshire Westwood ☎ 310/443 7000 🕐 Tue, Wed, Fri–Sat 11–7, Thu 11–9, Sun 11–5

California Museum of Science & Industry (► 50)
✉ 700 State Drive, Exposition Park ☎ 213/744 7400 🕐 Daily 10–5

Huntington Library, Art Gallery and Botanical Gardens (► 52)
✉ 1151 Oxford Road, San Marino ☎ 818/405 2100

Museum of Contemporary Art (MOCA) (► 53)
✉ 250 S Grand Avenue ☎ 213/621 2766

Museum of Tolerance
Interactive exhibits of hate activities (Holocaust, riots) designed to promote understanding.
✉ 9786 W Pico ☎ 310/553 9036 🕐 Mon–Thu 10–4, Fri 10–1, Sun 11–4

Rest of California

Monterey
Pacific House
Old West hotel and saloon-turned-museum.
✉ 10 Custom House Plaza ☎ 408/649 2907 🕐 Sep–May, daily 10–4; Jun–Aug, 10–5

Sacramento
Crocker Art Museum
Oldest art museum in the American West. European, Asian and California art in 19th-century building.
✉ 216 'O' Street ☎ 916/264 5423 🕐 Thu 10–9, Wed–Sun 10–5. Closed December

Concert Halls

San Francisco
Louise M Davies Symphony Hall
Symphonies, concerts; also tours of this fine stream-lined glass-and-granite building.
✉ Van Ness Avenue and Grove Street, Civic Center ☎ 510/864 6000

Los Angeles
Hollywood Bowl
Outdoor arena, year-round headline concerts of every music style, especially the LA Philharmonic.
✉ 2301 N Highland Avenue, Hollywood ☎ 213/850 2000

Wiltern Theatre
Intimate, acoustically wonderful hall features top-name musical performances in the art deco Wiltern Center.
✉ Wilshire and Western ☎ 213/480 3232

San Diego
Civic Theatre
Ultramodern design provides a great backdrop to concerts held here.

✉ San Diego Concourse, 202 'C' Street ☎ 619/236 6510

Nightlife

San Francisco
Finocchio's
Famous for its female impersonators. Three shows Wednesday to Sunday. Cover, 2-drink minimum, 21 and over.

✉ 506 Broadway, North Beach
☎ 415/982 9388

Vesuvio Cafe
This former haunt of Beat poets hasn't changed much in 30 years.

✉ 255 Columbus Avenue
☎ 415/362 3370

Los Angeles
The Baked Potato
Oldest major contemporary jazz club in California. Big-name entertainment for a moderate cost.

✉ 3787 Cahuenga Boulevard W, North Hollywood ☎ 818/980 1615

Bar Mamont
Intimate French colonial café, usually full of celebrities and paparazzi.

✉ 8171 Sunset Boulevard, Hollywood ☎ 213/650 0575

BB King's Blues Club
Three floors. Lucille's room is acoustic on Fri and Sat.

✉ 1000 Universal City Drive, Universal City ☎ 818/622 5464

Cat & Fiddle Pub and Restaurant
Ambient outdoor patio. Sunday jazz jam. No cover.

✉ 6530 Sunset Hollywood
☎ 323/468 3800

Cowboy Palace Saloon
The last real honky tonk in California. Live country seven nights. Pool, darts, dance classes. No cover.

✉ 21635 Devonshire Street, Chatsworth

Good Luck Bar
Knocked out of the No 1 spot by Bar Marmont, but now you finally have room to dance and enjoy yourself.

✉ 1514 Hillhurst Avenue, Los Feliz ☎ 213/666 3524

The Improvisation (Improv)
Site of *Live from the Improv* television show. Reservations.

✉ 8162 Melrose, West Hollywood ☎ 213/651 2583

Molly Malone's Irish Pub
Small neighbourhood bar with Irish folk, rock & roll, R & B nightly. Cover varies.

✉ 575 S Fairfax ☎ 213/935 1577

Rage
Gay/lesbian meeting place, alternative/underground music.

✉ 8911 Santa Monica Boulevard, West Hollywood
☎ 310/652 7055

Sidewalk Cafe
Live blues, country, reggae Tuesday through Sunday.

✉ 1401 Ocean Front Walk, Venice ☎ 310/399 5547

San Diego
Top O' the Cove
Piano bar/restaurant featuring show tunes and standards.

✉ 1216 Prospect Street, La Jolla ☎ 619/454 7779

Out on the Town
Karaoke's hot, but there's no lack of other choices for night-time entertainment in California: headline concerts to acoustical folk by local solo artists, poetry-readings to comedy, dramatic plays and musicals to raunchy revues. Even in the small communities, you can find live entertainment, with country music being the most popular. Parking can be difficult in Los Angeles, but valet parking is available at a reasonable cost.

Nightlife/Performing Arts Theatres/Sports

Pro Sports
For those who would rather watch than participate, pro sports are abundant in the state. Besides pro golf tours, there are several renowned horse-racing parks, especially Del Mar, a beachside track just north of San Diego. San Diego has pro baseball and football; LA has Clippers and Lakers basketball, baseball and hockey; San Diego has baseball, football, soccer and ice hockey. Information can be obtained from team offices. College sports add elan to the mix.

Nightlife

Rest of California

Eureka
Lost Coast Brewery & Café
Microbreweries are the rage, and this is one of the best.
✉ **617 Fourth Street**
☎ **707/445 4480**

Sacramento
Harlow's
Most glamorous nightclub in town. Upstairs is Momo's cigar lounge.
✉ **2708 'J' Street** ☎ **916/441 4693**

The Monkey Bar
Favourite haunt of the hip. Arrive early if you want to sit.
✉ **2730 Capitol Avenue**
☎ **916/442 8490**

Sunrise at the Oasis
Vegas-style theme bar, tastefully outrageous.
✉ **7811 Madison Avenue, Citrus Heights** ☎ **916/966 6274**

Performing Arts/Theatres

San Francisco
Orpheum Theatre
The largest touring shows to San Francisco play here.
✉ **1192 Market Street**
☎ **510/474 3800**

American Conservatory Theater (ACT)
One of the top regional theatres in the US.
✉ **415 Geary Street**
☎ **415/749 2228**

Los Angeles
Music Center of Los Angeles County
Includes Dorothy Chandler Pavilion, site of Academy Awards festivities; Mark Taper Forum, featuring experiment plays; and the Ahmanson, with musical comedies.
✉ **135 N Grand, downtown**
☎ **213/972 7211**

San Diego
Lawrence Welk Resort Theatre
Dinner theatre, with Broadway and Broadway-style shows. Buffet matinee and evening.
✉ **8860 Lawrence Welk Drive, Escondido** ☎ **619/749 3448**

Sledgehammer Theatre
Avant-garde productions.
✉ **1620 Sixth Avenue**
☎ **619/544 1484**

Rest of California

Orange County
Orange County Performing Arts Center
Regular performances by New York City Opera, American Ballet Theater and Los Angeles Philharmonic Orchestra, plus present-ations of popular musicals.
✉ **600 Town Center Drive, Costa Mesa** ☎ **714/556 2787**

Spectator Sports

Los Angeles
Wild Bill's Wild West Extravaganza
Two-hour Old West show with audience participation.
✉ **7600 Beach Boulevard, Buena Park** ☎ **714/522 6414**

Indio
Eldorado Polo Club
The 'Winter Polo Capital of the West'. Weekday practice matches are free. Picnic grounds.
✉ **50–950 Madison Street**
☎ **619/342 2223**

Monterey
Laguna Seca Raceway
Four major auto races a year, including restored antique cars.

✉ **1021 Monterey Road, Salinas 93908** ☎ **408/648 5100**

Sports

San Francisco
Several companies along the wharf offer sailing, fishing excursions and boat rentals. Some off-pier fishing as well.

Los Angeles
Hollywood Athletic Club
A huge room of full-sized vintage billiards tables; attracts the hip of Hollywood.

✉ **6525 W Sunset Boulevard, Hollywood** ☎ **213/962 6600**

Ice Capades Chalet Center
One of four indoor ice rinks in the LA area.

✉ **6100 Laurel Canyon Boulevard** ☎ **213/461 5400**

Moonlight Rollerway
Moonlight is one of the more popular indoor roller-blading rinks in LA.

✉ **5110 San Fernando Road, Glendale** ☎ **818/241 3630**

Sports Center Bowl
The landmark Jerry's Deli is right next door for a snack, after you've worked up an appetite.

✉ **12655 Ventura Boulevard, Studio City** ☎ **818/769 7600**
🕐 Call for open bowling hours

Rest of California

Lake Tahoe
Ski Lake Tahoe Association
Package deals available on the 15 downhill and 11 cross-country ski areas. Free shuttle between all.

☎ **916/544 7747 (Lake Tahoe Water Ski School)** for water ski details

Monterey
Monterey Bay Kayaks
Kayak rentals, tours.

✉ **693 Del Monte Avenue**
☎ **408/373 5357**

Palm Springs
Mission Hills Resort Golf Club
One reason Palm Springs is 'Winter Golf Capital of the World'.

✉ **71–501 Dinah Shore Drive, Rancho Mirage** ☎ **773/328 3198**

Palm Springs Tennis Center
Nine lighted courts open to the public.

✉ **1300 Baristo Road**
☎ **619/320 0020**

Pebble Beach
Spyglass Hill
Less expensive than Pebble Beach course (which hosts the AT&T ProAm tour), the bordering Pacific and Del Monte Forest make this difficult but scenic. Reserve a month in advance (year for groups).

✉ **Spyglass Hill Road**
☎ **408/624 3811**

Solvang
Windhaven Glider
Breathtaking glider rides

✉ **Santa Ynez Airport** ☎
805/688 8390 🕐 **10–5 daily**

Yosemite
Try rock-climbing, backpacking, camping, and hiking, guided or not. Sheer El Capitan mountain at 3,500 feet, attracts world-class climbers in search of a challenge.

Choices .
California offers the unique opportunity to visit multiple environments, all within a 24-hour period. You can spend the morning backpacking in the desert, the afternoon riding horses on wooded mountain trails, then head for the ocean for clam-digging or shell-hunting, and a sail into the sunset. For something different, cruise over to Mexico for some fast-paced jai alai (Fronton Palacio, ☎ 619/298 4105).

What's On When

The following are just a few of California's myriad festivals and celebrations.

January
Tournament of Roses Parade, Pasadena
Palm Springs International Film Festival

February
Chinese New Year Celebration, San Francisco
Napa Valley Mustard Celebration, Napa

March
International Asian Film Festival, San Francisco
Mendocino Whale Festival

April
Wine Country Celebration, Yountville
Toyota Grand Prix, Long Beach
Cherry Blossom Festival, San Francisco
Palm Desert Springfest, Palm Desert
Cinco De Mayo Celebration, state-wide

May
San Francisco International Film Fest
Muscle Car Show, Bakersfield
Sacramento Jazz Jubilee

June
Scottish Highlands Games and Gathering of the Clans, Modesto
Amador County Wine Festival, Plymouth
Sonoma Valley Shakespeare Festival, Sonoma

July
Festival of Arts and Pageant of the Masters, Laguna Beach
California Rodeo, Salinas
Greek Festival, Santa Barbara

August
Mozart Festival, San Luis Obispo
Sawdust Festival, Laguna Beach
San Francisco Mime Troupe Summer Park Season
Old Spanish Days Fiesta, Santa Barbara
Japanese Cultural Bazaar, Sacramento
California State Fair, Sacramento
Children's Festival of the Arts, Hollywood

September
Greek Food Festival, Sacramento
Oktoberfest, Huntington Beach
Danish Days, Solvang
Monterey Jazz Festival, Monterey
Armenian Food Festival, San Francisco
Bowlful of Blues Festival, Ojai
California International Air Show, Salinas

October
Grape Harvest Festival, Ontario
Jazz Festival, San Francisco
Rose Show, Santa Barbara

November
West Coast Ragtime Festival, Fresno
Christmas Parade, Hollywood

December
America's Tallest Living Christmas Tree, Ferndale
Newport Harbor Christmas Boat Parade, Newport Beach
Celebrity Cooks and Kitchens Tour, Mendocino

Practical Matters

Above: *T-shirts at Venice Beach*
Right: *having fun on the Boardwalk at Santa Cruz, a traditional American seaside resort*

TIME DIFFERENCES

GMT	California	Germany	USA (NY)	Netherlands	Spain
12 noon	← 4AM	→ 1PM	← 7AM	→ 1PM	→ 1PM

BEFORE YOU GO

WHAT YOU NEED

● Required
○ Suggested
▲ Not required

	UK	Germany	USA	Netherlands	Spain
Passport	●	●	▲	●	●
Visa	▲	▲	▲	▲	▲
Onward or Return Ticket	●	●	▲	●	●
Health Inoculations	▲	▲	▲	▲	▲
Health Documentation (► 123, Health)	●	●	●	●	●
Travel Insurance	○	○	○	○	○
Driving Licence (national)	●	●	●	●	●
Car Insurance Certificate (if own car)	○	○	○	○	○
Car Registration Document (if own car)	●	●	●	●	●

WHEN TO GO

San Francisco

High season

Low season

13°C	14°C	17°C	18°C	19°C	21°C	22°C	22°C	23°C	22°C	18°C	14°C
JAN	FEB	MAR	APR	MAY	JUN	JUL	AUG	SEP	OCT	NOV	DEC

 Very wet Wet Cloud Sun

TOURIST OFFICES

In the UK
Visit USA Association
☎ 0891 600 530
(24-hour recorded information and brochure request line only.

In the USA
United States Travel & Tourism Administration, 14th and Constitution Avenue NW, Washington DC 20230 ☎ 202/482 3811or 482 2000; fax 202/ 482 2887.

California Division of Tourism, 801 K Street, Suite 1600, Sacramento, CA 95812 ☎ 916/322 2881, call-free 800/862 2543; fax: 916/322 3402

POLICE 911

FIRE 911

AMBULANCE 911

WHEN YOU ARE THERE

ARRIVING

International direct flights operate into Los Angeles
(☎ 310/646 5252) – one of the world's busiest airports
– and San Francisco (☎ 415/721 0800). San Diego
Airport also has international flights but most stop en
route first. Charter flights also use these airports.

Los Angeles Airport
Miles to city centre

15 miles

Journey times	
🚌	45–60 minutes
🚌	35 minutes
🚗	30 minutes

San Francisco Airport
Miles to city centre

16 miles

Journey times	
🚌	N/A
🚌	30–60 minutes
🚗	30 minutes

MONEY

The American monetary unit is the dollar ($), which is
divided into 100 cents. There are coins of 1 cent
(penny), 5 cents (nickel), 10 cents (dime), 25 cents
(quarter), 50 cents (half dollar) and 1 dollar. Notes
(bills) are in denominations of 1, 2, 5, 10, 20, 50 and 100
dollars. Be warned, though: all notes, whatever their
value, are *exactly the same colour (green) and size.*

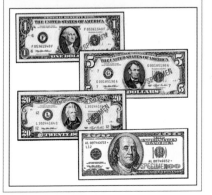

TIME

California is on
Pacific Standard
Time; eight hours
behind Greenwich Mean
Time (GMT-8), but from early
April, when clocks are put
forward one hour, to late
October, Daylight Saving
Time (GMT-7) operates.
California is also three hours
behind the east coast of the
USA (Eastern Standard
Time).

CUSTOMS

YES

**Goods Obtained Duty Free
for Import into the USA:**
Alcohol (spirits): 1L
Cigarettes: 200 *or*
Cigars (not Cuban): 50 *or*
Tobacco: 4.4 pounds (*or*
proportionate amounts of
each).
Gifts up to the value of $100
(including 100 cigars in
addition to the tobacco
allowance above); only for
non-US residents and may
only be claimed once in six
months.
(You must be 21 and over to
benefit from the alcohol
allowance and over 17 for
the tobacco allowance.)

NO

Drugs, firearms, ammunition,
offensive weapons, explo-
sives, obscene material,
some foods and agricultural
items.

CONSULATES

UK
310/477 3322 (LA)
415/981 3030 (SF)

Germany
213/930 2703 (LA)
415 775 1061 (SF)

Netherlands
310 268 1598 (LA)

Spain
213/938 0158 (LA)
415 922 2995 (SF)

WHEN YOU ARE THERE

TOURIST OFFICES

- Anaheim/ Orange County Visitor & Convention Bureau, 800 West Katella Avenue, Anaheim, CA 92802, ☎ 714/999 8999

- California Deserts Tourism Association, 37–115 Palm View Road, Rancho Mirage, CA 92270, ☎ 619/328 9256

- Los Angeles Convention & Visitors Bureau, 633 West Fifth Street, Suite 6000, Los Angeles, CA 90071, ☎ 213/624 7300

- Monterey Peninsula Visitors & Convention Bureau, 380 Alvarado Street, PO Box 1770, Monterey, CA 93940, ☎ 408/649 1770

- Palm Springs Tourism, 401 South Pavilion Way, Palm Springs, CA 92264, ☎ 773/778 8415

- Sacramento Convention & Visitors Bureau, 1421 K Street, Sacramento, CA 95814, ☎ 916/264 7777

- San Diego Convention & Visitors Bureau, 401 B Street, Suite 1400, San Diego, CA 92101, ☎ 619/236 1212

- San Francisco Convention & Visitors Bureau, 201 Third Street, Suite 900, San Francisco, CA 94103, ☎ 415/974 6900

NATIONAL HOLIDAYS

J	F	M	A	M	J	J	A	S	O	N	D
2	2			1		1		2	1	2	1

1 Jan	New Year's Day
Jan (3rd Mon)	Martin Luther King Jr's Birthday
12 Feb	Lincoln's Birthday
Feb (3rd Mon)	Washington's Birthday
May (last Mon)	Memorial Day
4 Jul	Independence Day
Sep (1st Mon)	Labor Day
9 Sep	Admission Day
Oct (2nd Mon)	Columbus Day
11 Nov	Veteran's Day
Nov (4th Thu)	Thanksgiving Day
25 Dec	Christmas Day

On these days shops, banks and businesses close.

OPENING HOURS

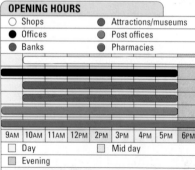

- ○ Shops
- ● Offices
- ● Banks
- ● Attractions/museums
- ● Post offices
- ● Pharmacies

| 9AM | 10AM | 11AM | 12PM | 2PM | 3PM | 4PM | 5PM | 6PM |

- □ Day
- □ Mid day
- ▨ Evening

In addition to the times shown above, many shops, particularly department stores within shopping malls, are open evenings and during afternoons on Sunday. Some supermarkets and grocery shops open 24 hours. Banks open until 5.30PM Friday and some major banks open on Saturday. Banks in some major towns and tourist areas may have longer hours. Some pharmacies open from 7AM to 9PM or even midnight, while some open 24 hours. Opening times of attractions and museums vary (see individual entries in the What to See section). Some post offices open Saturday 8AM–1PM.

DRIVE ON THE RIGHT

TOILETS FREE

PUBLIC TRANSPORT

Internal Flights Flying is the quickest way of getting around California and is not all that expensive if you take advantage of deals offered by airlines. The international airports of San Francisco, Oakland, Los Angeles and San Diego connect with a number of regional airports.

Trains Rail service is provided by America's National Railroad Corporation, Amtrak, which serves 72 California cities and towns. Carriages are clean, comfortable and rarely crowded. A Far Western Region Rail Pass (available only outside the US) gives 45 days unlimited travel over the far Western states.

Long Distance Buses Buses are by far the cheapest way of getting around. Greyhound Lines operates an inter-city service and also links many smaller towns within California. The Ameripass (only available outside the US) gives 4, 5, 7, 15, 30 or 60 days unlimited travel throughout the USA.

Ferries A ferry service links San Francisco with the Bay communities of Sausalito, Larkspur and Tiburon in scenic Marin County, and to Vallejo, Oakland and Alameda (departures from Pier 1, foot of Market Street). There is also a boat service from Long Beach and Newport Beach to Catalina Island.

Urban Transport Local communities and major cities are served by local bus services. In addition, San Francisco has cable-cars serving the downtown area and the BART train system covering the Bay areas. Los Angeles has its metrorail and San Diego has a trolley car service through the downtown area.

CAR RENTAL

If planning to rent a car, consider the fly/drive programmes many airline offer before you go. Other-wise most car rental companies have offices throughout the state. Charges depend on size of car, locale and time of year. Pay by credit card to avoid hefty cash deposit.

TAXIS

Taxis may be hailed on the street but few cruise outside tourist areas. If you are away from airports or major hotels it is best to phone for one (look under 'cabs' in Yellow Pages). In most cities rates are high, except San Francisco because of its comparatively small size.

DRIVING

Speed limits on rural interstate roads (motorways): **70mph**

Speed limits on many freeways (two-lane or more carriageways): **65mph**

Speed limits in residential and business districts and school zones: **25mph (or as signposted)**

Must be worn in front seats at all times and in rear seats where fitted.

Random breath-testing is frequent. Limit: 0.08 per cent alcohol.

Petrol (gasoline or gas), leaded and unleaded, is sold in US gallons (3.8 litres). Most petrol stations are self service. When removing the nozzle from the pump you must lift or turn the lever to activate it. Petrol is more expensive in remote areas and you may be charged more if paying by credit card.

If you break down in a rented car, phone the emergency number on the dashboard. Summon help from emergency telephones located along freeways (every ½ mile) and remote highways (every 2 miles), or sit tight and wait for the cruising highway patrol or state patrol to spot you (a raised bonnet should help).

PERSONAL SAFETY

California is certainly not crime free, but drugs are a problem, but exercise due caution, especially in downtown areas, and you should be safe. Away from these areas crime is quite low key. Some precautions:

- Do not peer at a map at every street corner, suggesting you are a lost tourist.
- If confronted by a mugger, hand over your money.
- If driving do not stop the car in any unlit or deserted urban area.

Police assistance:
☎ **911**
from any call box

TELEPHONES

Telephones are located in hotel and motel lobbies, drugstores, restaurants, garages and in roadside kiosks. Exact change in 5, 10 and 25 cent pieces is required to place a call. For internal calls dial 1 before the number when the area code is different from the one on the phone you are using. For the operator dial 0, for directory assistance dial 411.

International Dialling Codes

From the USA to:	
UK:	011 44
Germany:	011 49
Netherlands:	011 31
Spain:	011 34

POST

Post Offices
Post offices are plentiful in cities. Stamps are also sold from stamp machines in hotels and shops but have a 25 per cent mark up. Main post offices in larger cities open 24 hours, otherwise hours are: 8–6 (noon Sat). Closed: Sun. ☎ 213/617 4543 (LA); ☎ 415/441 0329 (San Fran)

ELECTRICITY

The power supply is: 110–115 volts

Round 3-hole sockets taking plugs with 2 flat pins in a parallel position, with an upper, round, earth pin for earthed appliances. European visitors should bring a voltage transformer as well as an adaptor.

TIPS/GRATUITIES

Yes ✓ No ✗		
Restaurants	✓	15–20%
Cafeterias/fast-food outlets	✗	
Bars	✓	15–20%
Taxis	✓	15–20%
Porters	✓	$1/bag
Chambermaids	✓	$1/day
Usherettes	✗	
Hairdressers	✓	$1–2
Cloakroom attendants	✓	$1/coat
Toilets	✗	

PHOTOGRAPHY

What to photograph: alpine ranges, redwood forests, thundering rivers, crystal-clear lakes, spectacular deserts, sunny beaches, glitzy cities.
Where to buy film: drugstores and supermarkets are probably the cheapest places; you will pay more at specialised kiosks near major tourist attractions.
Video film: the format used for video cassettes in the US differs from that used in the UK. You cannot buy videos in the US compatible with a video camera bought in the UK.

HEALTH

Insurance
There is no agreement for medical treatment between the US and other countries and all travellers MUST be covered by medical insurance (for an unlimited amount of medical costs is advisable). Treatment will be refused without evidence of insurance.

Dental Services
Medical insurance (see above) will cover you for dental treatment. In the event of any emergency, see your hotel concierge or consult the Yellow Pages for an emergency dentist.

Sun Advice
California enjoys a lot of sunshine with more than 250 clear days a year. Along the coast mornings can be hazily overcast and sea breezes (especially in the north) can make it feel cooler than it is. Protect the skin at all times.

Drugs
Quick-remedy medicines such as aspirin are readily available at any pharmacy (drugstore). For tablets containing acetaminophen read paracetamol. Also, many pain-killing pills available 'over the counter' at home may need a prescription in the US.

Safe Water
It is quite safe to drink tap water. In hotels and restaurants a nice touch is that water, generally ice cold, is provided free with meals. Bottled water is also widely available but is not as popular as in Europe.

CONCESSIONS

Students Upon production of ID proving student status, there are discounts available on travel, theatre and museum tickets, plus at some nightspots. It is always worth asking at the outset.

Senior Citizens For anyone over the age of 62 there is a tremendous variety of discounts on offer (upon proof of age). Both Amtrak (train) and Greyhound (bus), as well as many US airlines, offer (smallish) percentage reductions on fares. Museums, art galleries, attractions, cinemas, and even hotels offer small discounts, and as the definition of senior can drop to as low as 55, it is always worth enquiring.

CLOTHING SIZES

USA	UK	Europe	
36	36	46	Suits
38	38	48	
40	40	50	
42	42	52	
44	44	54	
46	46	56	
8	7	41	Shoes
8.5	7.5	42	
9.5	8.5	43	
10.5	9.5	44	
11.5	10.5	45	
12	11	46	
14.5	14.5	37	Shirts
15	15	38	
15.5	15.5	39/40	
16	16	41	
16.5	16.5	42	
17	17	43	
6	8	34	Dresses
8	10	36	
10	12	38	
12	14	40	
14	16	42	
16	18	44	
6	4.5	38	Shoes
6.5	5	38	
7	5.5	39	
7.5	6	39	
8	6.5	40	
8.5	7	41	

- Contact the airport or airline the day prior to leaving to ensure flight details are unchanged.
- Departure tax: all airport, customs and security taxes are included in the price of the ticket.
- Check the duty-free limits of the country you are entering before departure.

LANGUAGE

English is the official language of the USA. Californians, however, are a fascinating mix of cultures, most notably of Spanish or Mexican extraction. In fact, Spanish is heard throughout California. Spanish is met in many forms, for instance in city and street names. The five largest cities in California: Los Angeles, San Diego, San Francisco, San Jose and Sacramento bear Spanish names. However, although English is the native language there are many differences between its British and American usage. Some of the more commonly encountered are listed below:

holiday	*vacation*	tap	*faucet*
fortnight	*two weeks*	refrigerator	*icebox*
ground floor	*first floor*	luggage	*baggage*
first floor	*second floor*	suitcase	*valise*
second floor	*third floor*	hotel porter	*bellhop*
flat	*apartment*	chambermaid	*room maid*
lift	*elevator*	surname	*last name*
eiderdown	*comforter*	cupboard	*closet*

cheque	*check*	25 cent coin	*quarter*
traveller's cheque	*traveler's check*	banknote	*bill*
		banknote (colloquial)	*greenback*
1 cent coin	*penny*		
5 cent coin	*nickel*	dollar (colloquial)	*buck*
10 cent coin	*dime*	cashpoint	*automatic teller*

grilled	*broiled*	biscuit	*cookie*
frankfurter	*frank*	scone	*biscuit*
prawns	*shrimp*	sorbet	*sherbet*
aubergine	*eggplant*	jelly	*jello*
courgette	*zucchini*	jam	*jelly*
maize	*corn*	confectionery	*candy*
chips (potato)	*fries*	spirit	*liquor*
crisps (potato)	*chips*	soft drink	*soda*

car	*automobile*	petrol	*gas, gasoline*
bonnet (of car)	*hood*	railway	*railroad, railway*
boot (of car)	*trunk*	tram	*streetcar*
repair	*fix*	underground	*subway*
caravan	*trailer*	platform	*track*
lorry	*truck*	buffer	*bumper*
motorway	*freeway*	single ticket	*one-way ticket*
main road	*highway*	return ticket	*round-trip ticket*

shop	*store*	policeman	*cop*
chemist (shop)	*drugstore*	post	*mail*
cinema	*movies*	post code	*zip code*
pavement	*sidewalk*	ring up, telephone	*call*
subway	*underpass*		
gangway	*aisle*	long-distance call	*trunk call*
toilet	*rest room*		
trousers	*pants*	autumn	*fall*
nappy	*diaper*	gangway	*aisle*
glasses	*eyeglasses*	pavement	*sidewalk*

Acknowledgements
The Automobile Association wishes to thank the following libraries, photographers and associations for
their assistance in the preparation of this book.

© DISNEY ENTERPRISES, INC. 18; MARY EVANS 10; RONALD GRANT ARCHIVE 11, 14; ROBERT
HARDING 22, ROBERT HOLMES 8a, 31, 44, 62, 63, 64, 67, 87, 88, 89; MRI BANKER'S GUIDE TO
FOREIGN CURRENCY 119; PICTURES COLOUR LIBRARY 9b; SPECTRUM COLOUR LIBRARY F/cover
(a): Yosemite, 27a, 56, 58.
The remaining transparencies are held in the Association's own library (**AA PHOTO LIBRARY**) and were
taken by H Harris B/cover: grapes, 15b, 24; R Holmes 2, 6, 7, 8b, 12, 16, 17, 19, 20, 22/3, 25, 26, 35, 36,
38, 39, 40b, 41a, 43, 49, 50, 55, 57, 59, 60, 61, 65, 66, 71a, 71b, 72, 73, 74, 75, 76/7, 81, 82, 83, 84, 85,
86, 90, 91a, 117b, 122a; K Patterson F/cover (b): Harley Davidson, 13, 27b, 33, 34, 37, 40a, 41b, 42, 80a,
91b, 117a, 122b, 122c; B Smith 32; P Wood F/cover (c): rollerblader, 1, 5a, 5b, 9a, 15a, 21, 45, 48, 51, 52,
53, 54, 79, 80b.

Author's Acknowledgements
Richard Minnich wishes to thank Mr and Mrs Fred B Minnich, Ms Karen Hicks, Dr and Mrs John L
Graves, the Los Angeles branch of the California Film Commission and Mr and Mrs Brian Kaminer for
their help with this book.

Contributors
Copy editor: Larry Dunmire   **Page Layout:** Design 23   **Verifier:** Sheila Hawkins
Researcher (Practical Matters): Colin Follett   **Indexer:** Marie Lorimer